The Spokesman
Extraordinary Rendition
Edited by Ken Coates

Published by Spokesman for the
Bertrand Russell Peace Foundation

Spokesman 89   2006

CONTENTS

Editorial	3	Ken Coates
I Imperial Overreach		
II A Case to Answer		
Art, Truth & Politics	8	Harold Pinter
Extraordinary Rendition	19	Ken Coates
Case Studies		
I Maher Arar's story	26	
II Abu Omar's story	34	
III Khaled El-Masri's story	41	
IV Omar Deghayes' story	47	Jackie Chase
V Soldiers out of Control	49	Human Rights Watch
VI Privatised Interrogation	59	Pratap Chatterjee
'The US does not condone …'	64	Condoleezza Rice / Andrew Tyrie MP
American Prisoners in Europe	70	Human Rights Watch / Dick Marty, Council of Europe
Precedents for Torture	74	Naomi Klein
Rendition is Abduction	78	Lord Steyn interviewed by Jon Snow
Who Fooled America?	82	Lawrence Wilkerson
Dossier	85	Israel's heavy water / International Criminal Court / What happened in Greece? / Terrorism Bill – worrying precedent
Reviews	90	Michael Barratt Brown / John Daniels / Tony Simpson

Printed by the Russell Press Ltd., Nottingham, UK

ISSN 0262 7922   ISBN 0 85124 722 9

Subscriptions
Institutions £30.00/€60/$60
Individuals £20.00 (UK)
    £25.00 (ex UK)
    €40/$40

Back issues available on request

A CIP catalogue record for this book is available from the British Library

Published by the
Bertrand Russell Peace Foundation Ltd.,
Russell House
Bulwell Lane
Nottingham NG6 0BT
England
Tel. 0115 9784504
email:
elfeuro@compuserve.com
www.spokesmanbooks.com
www.russfound.org

Editorial Board:
Michael Barratt Brown
Ken Coates
John Daniels
Ken Fleet
Stuart Holland
Tony Simpson

BERTRAND RUSSELL

Get inside one of the greatest minds of the 20th Century

'There is no one who uses the English language more beguilingly than Russell, no one smoothes the kinks and creases more artfully out of the most crumpled weaves of thought.' – *The Times*

ABC of Relativity
Bertrand Russell
Introduction by **Peter Clark**

Bertrand Russell's most brilliant work of scientific popularisation.

Pb: 0-415-15429-4: £11.99

The Scientific Outlook
Bertrand Russell

This early classic illuminates Russell's thinking on the promise and threat of scientific progress.

Hb: 0-415-24996-1: £50.00
Pb: 0-415-24997-X: £13.99

The Collected Papers of Bertrand Russell Volume 29
Détente or Destruction, 1955-57
Bertrand Russell
Edited by **Andrew G. Bone**

Continues the publication of Routledge's multi-volume critical edition of Bertrand Russell's shorter writings.

February 2005
Hb: 0-415-35837-X: £125.00

Common Sense and Nuclear Warfare
Bertrand Russell
Introduction by
Ken Coates

This book presents Russell's keen insights into the threat of nuclear conflict, and his argument that the only way to end this threat is to end war itself.

Hb: 0415249945: £50.00
Pb: 0415249953: £9.99

Power
A New Social Analysis
Bertrand Russell
Introduction by
Samuel Brittan

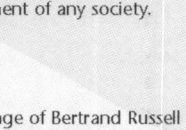

In this remarkable book Russell argues that power is man's ultimate goal and is, in its many guises, the single most important element in the development of any society.

Routledge Classics series
Pb: 0-415-32507-2: £9.99

For details on our full range of Bertrand Russell titles, and how to order, please visit
www.routledge.com

For credit card orders: call +44 (0)1264 343071
or email book.orders@routledge.co.uk
For more information, or for a free Philosophy catalogue please call
Helen Lawton on 020 7017 6044 or email helen.lawton@tandf.co.uk

Editorial

I: Imperial Overreach

Three thousand four hundred British troops are shortly to be sent to Southern Afghanistan to the province of Helmand. They will be part of a six thousand-strong Nato force announced on 8th December 2005. As they go in, some four thousand Americans will withdraw.

It was alleged that the war in Afghanistan was over in the year 2001. All the arts of the American Air Force had been deployed to complete the destruction of Kabul, begun by the Soviet Union. Bandits of all kinds were mustered in an army of desperadoes, which completed on the ground the labours of the airmen above it. Wholesale production of opium then resumed after the rout of the Taliban.

But the revival of the opium economy has hardly improved the polity. President Karzai rules some or even most of Kabul, rather uneasily and with the help of strong forces of bodyguards. The rest of the country seethes under the protection of a wide variety of narcotic entrepreneurs, tribal commanders and long established warlords. The Americans continue to maintain an outpost at Bagram, to man their torture facilities and to host the long-delayed nemesis of Osama bin Laden. They have no appetite, they tell us, for nation building: and indeed nation building is not the most attractive project for this territory, which has resolutely defeated earlier 'civilising' missions over the centuries, has already made a potent contribution to the downfall of the Soviet Union, and is busily engaged in aiding that of the United States of America.

It takes the political genius of Tony Blair to lead beleaguered remnants of the British Empire into a battle such as this, already so comprehensively lost by the major powers in the modern world.

The deployment announced by Adam Ingram in November 2005 has the objective of 'restoring Afghanistan as a secure and stable state, and preventing the country from again becoming a haven for global terrorists'. Here we go again.

The International Security Assistance Force is a wholly owned subsidiary of Nato, operating on the basis of very reluctantly accepted Jubilee decisions of that organisation to operate 'out of area'. The list of countries committed to such operations is very long. It begins with Albania, Austria and Azerbaijan, and it labours through the alphabet to Turkey, the United Kingdom and the United States of America. It took all Bill Clinton's wiles, and the experience of George Robertson as a compositor and stitcher-up of trade union motions, to patch together the agreement by Nato, to operate 'out of area'. So it came about that a total of nine thousand cosmopolitan troops found themselves deployed in the least hospitable parts of Afghanistan.

For most of the thirty-five participating nations, they have gone there under a token agreement, to dispatch minute numbers of qualified observers or specialists, ones or twos or tens, to endure the acute discomforts of life on the frontier. For those who have undertaken to do marginally more, the issue is highly contentious, and the Dutch are already involved in elaborate arguments about extricating themselves. French, Germans and Spaniards have undertaken responsibilities to maintain order in Kabul, but they have no appetite to extend the benefits of nationhood to the rest of the country, leave alone to turbulent Helmand, which is a hotbed of the re-emergent Taliban.

There is, of course, a powerful argument for dispatching an expeditionary force led by John Reid, the New Labour Minister of Defence, composed of all the Blair acolytes. Whatever else such a force might accomplish, it would probably generate, among the none-too-many survivors, a wholesome diminution of the appetite for imperial overreach. But it is difficult to see why normal British soldiers should deserve to be put through this experience.

New Labour has already eradicated the opium poppy crop once. It sent Clare Short to ensure that it was uprooted, at a time when six Afghan provinces were growing poppies. Now the UN tells us that there are twenty-eight provinces in which the poppies flourish, to the immense advantage of the heroin market around the world, particularly in Britain.

In *The Guardian* (4th January 2006) Simon Jenkins delivered a fitting response to this decision, characterising it as 'the half-baked product of Tony Blair's global machismo'. Henry McCubbin wrote to Simon Jenkins afterwards:

'I was pleased to see that you quoted from Tony Blair's 1999 Speech to the Chicago Chamber of Commerce in your article based on Britain's additional deployment to Afghanistan. Blair was not just setting down the limits of military deployment in that speech, he was recasting Britain's foreign policy as one based on militaristic solutions to international disputes. A point not often picked up by commentators.

Forewarnings of this change were made apparent within the Labour Party when Blair ditched Clause Four in 1995. The headline was Labour discarding its commitments to common ownership, but also contained within Clause Four were Labour's stated principles with regards to the resolution of international disputes. This laid down that the UN was to be the final arbiter in disputes between nations. The Blair Clause Four removed this commitment. The change was noticed and a group of Labour Members of the European Parliament, myself included, requested that the proposed text be amended to reinstate this commitment, but, alas, amendments were disallowed. Meantime the courtiers, who had already started to surround Blair, dismissed our views contemptuously, stating that we should have no fears that New Labour would become warmongers, and that we were being disloyal to the project by doubting the leader's integrity.

Nato's new "out of area role" now looks quite unachievable as the major powers back off humanitarian intervention, which by custom, practice and necessity has been driven to fall under the logic of the military who have been put in charge of such operations. To me it would appear that humanitarian intervention sees the skies darken with B-52s long before the ambulances and truckloads of aid appear.

But expect much more of this. The lifetime costs of Blair's greatest folly, the construction and equipping of two giant aircraft carriers at a lifetime cost of £31 billion, will have to be reviewed, just as Denis Healey had to do with aircraft carriers in the sixties. Their use can only be out of area, i.e. the poor, racially and culturally different south where we will, as in Joseph Conrad's novel, be projecting our imperial might by letting off loud explosions in the Heart of Darkness to remind the restless natives who is in charge.

Blair's 1999 speech is indeed seminal and has turned out to be deadly for many innocents. But try as you may, I defy you to find any serious writings or speeches on this subject prior to Blair becoming Leader of the Labour Party in 1994 or Prime Minister in 1997. He showed what can best be described as indifference to the subject until he met with the likes of Jonathan Powell.'

If those whom the Gods would destroy they first make mad, then the victims must be compelled to wonder why the gap between madness and destruction is so unconscionably long.

Ken Coates

II: A Case to Answer

In August 2004 Adam Price, MP, a leading spokesman of the Welsh Nationalists in Parliament, published a report on 'The potential impeachment of the Prime Minister for High Crimes and Misdemeanours in relation to the invasion of Iraq'. He quickly gained support from the Scottish Nationalists, with the powerful advocacy of Alex Salmond, MP. But then he attracted the attention of the Whips, whose shadow fell across the other Parties with varying efficiency. All the Labour Members were intimidated, and most of the Liberals and Conservatives. Some brave souls stood out, and were able to carry the argument further afield into the country.

In October 2004 we published the report as a little book. It had been written by Glen Rangwala and Dan Plesch, and maintained a consistently high level of argument. But high levels of argument do not necessarily wash away the bad intentions of the Whips, who have surely been reinforced in all their authoritarian biases by the results of the Iraq war.

Now, another brave voice speaks out. General Sir Michael Rose has published a strong appeal in *The Guardian*. It appeared under the headline 'Enough of his excuses: Blair must be impeached over Iraq' (January 10th 2006).

> 'Wars are won when the people, government and army work together for a common cause in which they genuinely believe. Whereas the people may be initially uncertain about military intervention, politicians will often be the strongest advocates – blinded by the imperatives of their political views. It will invariably be military commanders who are most cautious about using force – for they understand better than most the consequences of engaging in war.
>
> Although in a true democracy they must remain subordinate to their political masters, they have a clear responsibility to point out when political strategies are flawed or inadequately resourced. Since they might also have to ask their soldiers to sacrifice their lives, they must be assured that a war is just, legal and the last resort available. Yet three years ago this country was somehow led by the prime minister into war in Iraq where few, if any, of these requirements were met.

Most importantly a clear justification for the war in Iraq was never sufficiently made by Tony Blair – for the intelligence he presented was also embarrassingly patchy and inconsistent. What is more, his unequivocal statement to the House of Commons that Saddam Hussein possessed weapons of mass destruction that could be used within 45 minutes was made without being properly validated – for it was decided in Washington and London to launch the invasion of Iraq early, on the basis of the flimsy evidence available. This was done without asking the UN weapons inspectors, who were actually on the ground in Iraq, to investigate this allegation. Ultimately, as the inspectors suspected and as we now all know, it turned out that there were no such weapons. Britain had been led into war on false pretences. It was a war that was to unleash untold suffering on the Iraqi people and cause grave damage to the west's prospects in the wider war against global terror.

Nevertheless, today the Prime Minister seeks to persuade the world that the war was justifiable because Saddam Hussein was toppled and there now exists in Iraq a slender hope of democracy. The Iraqi elections are a creditable achievement by the coalition forces. But it must be remembered that a general election was previously held in Iraq in 1956, and within two years the country had fallen under military rule. Without adequate security and the necessary democratic institutions in place, there are absolutely no long-term guarantees that democracy will endure.

Before the invasion, regime change was never cited as a reason for going to war. Indeed, Mr. Blair insisted that regime change was not, nor ever could be, a reason for going to war. Had such a justification been fully debated in parliament, it is exceedingly unlikely that the necessary political support would have been forthcoming. It was the apparent need to defend ourselves against a dire threat – so vividly described by Mr. Blair in the Commons – that finally won the political argument.

During the build-up to war and since, most of the electorate of this country have consistently opposed the decision to invade. People have seen their political wishes ignored for reasons now proved false. But there has been no attempt in Parliament to call Mr. Blair personally to account for what has transpired to be a blunder of enormous strategic significance. It should come as no surprise therefore that so many of this country's voters have turned their backs on a democratic system they feel has so little credibility and is so unresponsive.

One obvious way of re-engaging these disaffected voters would be for Parliament to accept that it wrongly supported the war – but only because it believed what Mr. Blair told them. Now it is clear that Parliament was misled by Mr. Blair, either wittingly or unwittingly, Parliament should also call on him for a full explanation as to why he went to war. It is not a sufficient excuse for Mr. Blair to say that he acted in good faith and that his decisions were based on the intelligence he had been given. For it is the clear responsibility of people in his position to test intelligence. No intelligence can ever be taken at face value. Indeed it is negligent so to do.

Parliament should therefore ascertain how far the Prime Minister did evaluate intelligence regarding weapons of mass destruction and how he assessed the reliability of the many sources that provided that intelligence. It should ask him what corroborating evidence there was for his specific statement about weapons of mass destruction – and why more use was not made of the UN inspectors on the ground in Iraq to test the validity of that statement. It should inquire just how much he discounted the mass of intelligence that came in from the Iraqi National Congress – a body that had a vested interest in removing Saddam from power. The list of possible questions is huge and would no doubt be usefully expanded during any hearings.

Mr. Blair is an able barrister who should relish the opportunity to put his side of the case. No one can undo the decision to go to war. But the impeachment of Mr. Blair is now something I believe must happen if we are to rekindle interest in the democratic process.'

General Sir Michael Rose was adjutant general of the British Army and Commander of the UN Protection Force in Bosnia.

'A clear justification for the war in Iraq was never sufficiently made by Tony Blair ... No one can undo the decision to go to war. But the impeachment of Mr Blair is now something I believe must happen if we are to rekindle interest in the democratic process.'
General Sir Michael Rose in
The Guardian 10/1/06

A Case to Answer

A first report on the potential impeachment of the Prime Minister for High Crimes and Misdemeanours in relation to the invasion of Iraq
by Glen Rangwala & Dan Plesch for Adam Price MP

With Legal Opinion by
Rabinder Singh QC & Prof. Conor Gearty
Price: £6.00 inc. p&p

The Dodgiest Dossier

Brings together all the leaked memoranda about the British Government's decision to go to war on Iraq, plus the Attorney General's legal advice. These papers show in graphic detail how weak was the pre-war evidence for attacking Iraq.
Price £5 including p&p

Spokesman Books,

Russell House, Bulwell Lane, Nottingham, NG6 0BT, England
Tel: 0115 9708318 - Fax: 0115 9420433
Credit/Debit cards accepted - elfeuro@compuserve.com
www.spokesmanbooks.com

Art, Truth & Politics

Harold Pinter – Nobel Lecture

The Nobel Prize in Literature for 2005 was awarded to the writer Harold Pinter. He made his playwriting debut in 1957 with The Room, *presented in Bristol. Other early plays included* The Birthday Party *(1957) and* The Dumb Waiter *(1957). His conclusive breakthrough came with* The Caretaker *(1959), followed by* The Homecoming *(1964),* Landscape *(1967) and* Silence *(1968) and later, among others,* One for the Road *(1984),* Mountain Language *(1988), and* The New World Order *(1991).*

In 1958 I wrote the following:

'There are no hard distinctions between what is real and what is unreal, nor between what is true and what is false. A thing is not necessarily either true or false; it can be both true and false.'

I believe that these assertions still make sense and do still apply to the exploration of reality through art. So as a writer I stand by them but as a citizen I cannot. As a citizen I must ask: What is true? What is false?

Truth in drama is forever elusive. You never quite find it but the search for it is compulsive. The search is clearly what drives the endeavour. The search is your task. More often than not you stumble upon the truth in the dark, colliding with it or just glimpsing an image or a shape which seems to correspond to the truth, often without realising that you have done so. But the real truth is that there never is any such thing as one truth to be found in dramatic art. There are many. These truths challenge each other, recoil from each other, reflect each other, ignore each other, tease each other, are blind to each other. Sometimes you feel you have the truth of a moment in your hand, then it slips through your fingers and is lost.

I have often been asked how my plays come about. I cannot say. Nor can I ever sum up my plays, except to say that this is what happened. That is what they said. That is what they did.

Most of the plays are engendered by a line, a word or an image. The given word is often shortly followed by the image. I shall give two examples of two lines which came right out of the blue into my head, followed by an image, followed by me.

The plays are *The Homecoming* and *Old Times*. The first line of *The Homecoming* is 'What have you done with the scissors?' The first line of *Old Times* is 'Dark.'

In each case I had no further information.

In the first case someone was obviously looking for a pair of scissors and was demanding their whereabouts of someone else he suspected had probably stolen them. But I somehow knew that the person addressed didn't give a damn about the scissors or about the questioner either, for that matter.

'Dark' I took to be a description of someone's hair, the hair of a woman, and was the answer to a question. In each case I found myself compelled to pursue the matter. This happened visually, a very slow fade, through shadow into light.

I always start a play by calling the characters A, B and C.

In the play that became *The Homecoming* I saw a man enter a stark room and ask his question of a younger man sitting on an ugly sofa reading a racing paper. I somehow suspected that A was a father and that B was his son, but I had no proof. This was however confirmed a short time later when B (later to become Lenny) says to A (later to become Max), 'Dad, do you mind if I change the subject? I want to ask you something. The dinner we had before, what was the name of it? What do you call it? Why don't you buy a dog? You're a dog cook. Honest. You think you're cooking for a lot of dogs.' So since B calls A 'Dad' it seemed to me reasonable to assume that they were father and son. A was also clearly the cook and his cooking did not seem to be held in high regard. Did this mean that there was no mother? I didn't know. But, as I told myself at the time, our beginnings never know our ends.

'Dark.' A large window. Evening sky. A man, A (later to become Deeley), and a woman, B (later to become Kate), sitting with drinks. 'Fat or thin?' the man asks. Who are they talking about? But I then see, standing at the window, a woman, C (later to become Anna), in another condition of light, her back to them, her hair dark.

It's a strange moment, the moment of creating characters who up to that moment have had no existence. What follows is fitful, uncertain, even hallucinatory, although sometimes it can be an unstoppable avalanche. The author's position is an odd one. In a sense he is not welcomed by the characters. The characters resist him, they are not easy to live with, they are impossible to define. You certainly can't dictate to them. To a certain extent you play a never-ending game with them, cat and mouse, blind man's buff, hide and seek. But finally you find that you have people of flesh and blood on your hands, people with will and an individual sensibility of their own, made out of component parts you are unable to change, manipulate or distort.

So language in art remains a highly ambiguous transaction, a quicksand, a trampoline, a frozen pool which might give way under you, the author, at any time.

But as I have said, the search for the truth can never stop. It cannot be adjourned, it cannot be postponed. It has to be faced, right there, on the spot.

Political theatre presents an entirely different set of problems. Sermonising has to be avoided at all cost. Objectivity is essential. The characters must be allowed to breathe their own air. The author cannot confine and constrict them to satisfy his own taste or disposition or prejudice. He must be prepared to approach them from a variety of angles, from a full and uninhibited range of perspectives, take them by surprise, perhaps, occasionally, but nevertheless give them the freedom to go which way they will. This does not always work. And political satire, of course, adheres to none of these precepts, in fact does precisely the opposite, which is its proper function.

In my play *The Birthday Party* I think I allow a whole range of options to operate in a dense forest of possibility before finally focussing on an act of subjugation.

Mountain Language pretends to no such range of operation. It remains brutal, short and ugly. But the soldiers in the play do get some fun out of it. One sometimes forgets that torturers become easily bored. They need a bit of a laugh to keep their spirits up. This has been confirmed of course by the events at Abu Ghraib in Baghdad. *Mountain Language* lasts only 20 minutes, but it could go on for hour after hour, on and on and on, the same pattern repeated over and over again, on and on, hour after hour.

Ashes to Ashes, on the other hand, seems to me to be taking place under water. A drowning woman, her hand reaching up through the waves, dropping down out of sight, reaching for others, but finding nobody there, either above or under the water, finding only shadows, reflections, floating; the woman a lost figure in a drowning landscape, a woman unable to escape the doom that seemed to belong only to others.

But as they died, she must die too.

Political language, as used by politicians, does not venture into any of this territory since the majority of politicians, on the evidence available to us, are interested not in truth but in power and in the maintenance of that power. To maintain that power it is essential that people remain in ignorance, that they live in ignorance of the truth, even the truth of their own lives. What surrounds us therefore is a vast tapestry of lies, upon which we feed.

As every single person here knows, the justification for the invasion of Iraq was that Saddam Hussein possessed a highly dangerous body of weapons of mass destruction, some of which could be fired in 45 minutes, bringing about appalling devastation. We were assured that was true. It was not true. We were told that Iraq had a relationship with al Qaeda and shared responsibility for the atrocity in New York of September 11th 2001. We were assured that this was true. It was not true. We were told that Iraq threatened the security of the world. We were assured it was true. It was not true.

The truth is something entirely different. The truth is to do with how the United States understands its role in the world and how it chooses to embody it.

But before I come back to the present I would like to look at the recent past, by which I mean United States foreign policy since the end of the Second World War. I believe it is obligatory upon us to subject this period to at least some kind of even limited scrutiny, which is all that time will allow here.

Everyone knows what happened in the Soviet Union and throughout Eastern Europe during the post-war period: the systematic brutality, the widespread atrocities, the ruthless suppression of independent thought. All this has been fully documented and verified.

But my contention here is that the US crimes in the same period have only been superficially recorded, let alone documented, let alone acknowledged, let alone recognised as crimes at all. I believe this must be addressed and that the truth has considerable bearing on where the world stands now. Although constrained, to a certain extent, by the existence of the Soviet Union, the United States' actions throughout the world made it clear that it had concluded it had *carte blanche* to do what it liked.

Direct invasion of a sovereign state has never in fact been America's favoured method. In the main, it has preferred what it has described as 'low intensity conflict'. Low intensity conflict means that thousands of people die but slower than if you dropped a bomb on them in one fell swoop. It means that you infect the heart of the country, that you establish a malignant growth and watch the gangrene bloom. When the populace has been subdued – or beaten to death – the same thing – and your own friends, the military and the great corporations, sit comfortably in power, you go before the camera and say that democracy has prevailed. This was a commonplace in US foreign policy in the years to which I refer.

The tragedy of Nicaragua was a highly significant case. I choose to offer it here as a potent example of America's view of its role in the world, both then and now.

I was present at a meeting at the US Embassy in London in the late 1980s.

The United States Congress was about to decide whether to give more money to the Contras in their campaign against the state of Nicaragua. I was a member of a delegation speaking on behalf of Nicaragua but the most important member of this delegation was a Father John Metcalf. The leader of the US body was Raymond Seitz (then number two to the ambassador, later ambassador himself). Father Metcalf said: 'Sir, I am in charge of a parish in the north of Nicaragua. My parishioners built a school, a health centre, a cultural centre. We have lived in peace. A few months ago a Contra force attacked the parish. They destroyed everything: the school, the health centre, the cultural centre. They raped nurses and teachers, slaughtered doctors, in the most brutal manner. They behaved like savages. Please demand that the US government withdraw its support from this shocking terrorist activity.'

Raymond Seitz had a very good reputation as a rational, responsible and highly sophisticated man. He was greatly respected in diplomatic circles. He listened, paused and then spoke with some gravity. 'Father,' he said, 'let me tell you something. In war, innocent people always suffer.' There was a frozen silence. We stared at him. He did not flinch.

Innocent people, indeed, always suffer.

Finally somebody said: 'But in this case 'innocent people' were the victims of a gruesome atrocity subsidised by your government, one among many. If Congress allows the Contras more money further atrocities of this kind will take place. Is this not the case? Is your government not therefore guilty of supporting acts of murder and destruction upon the citizens of a sovereign state?'

Seitz was imperturbable. 'I don't agree that the facts as presented support your assertions,' he said.

As we were leaving the Embassy a US aide told me that he enjoyed my plays. I did not reply.

I should remind you that at the time President Reagan made the following statement: 'The Contras are the moral equivalent of our Founding Fathers.'

The United States supported the brutal Somoza dictatorship in Nicaragua for over 40 years. The Nicaraguan people, led by the Sandinistas, overthrew this regime in 1979, a breathtaking popular revolution.

The Sandinistas weren't perfect. They possessed their fair share of arrogance and their political philosophy contained a number of contradictory elements. But they were intelligent, rational and civilised. They set out to establish a stable, decent, pluralistic society. The death penalty was abolished. Hundreds of thousands of poverty-stricken peasants were brought back from the dead. Over 100,000 families were given title to land. Two thousand schools were built. A quite remarkable literacy campaign reduced illiteracy in the country to less than one seventh. Free education was established and a free health service. Infant mortality was reduced by a third. Polio was eradicated.

The United States denounced these achievements as Marxist/Leninist subversion. In the view of the US government, a dangerous example was being set. If Nicaragua was allowed to establish basic norms of social and economic justice, if it was allowed to raise the standards of health care and education and achieve social unity and national self respect, neighbouring countries would ask the same questions and do the same things. There was of course at the time fierce resistance to the status quo in El Salvador.

I spoke earlier about 'a tapestry of lies' which surrounds us. President Reagan commonly described Nicaragua as a 'totalitarian dungeon'. This was taken generally by the media, and certainly by the British government, as accurate and fair comment. But there was in fact no record of death squads under the Sandinista government. There was no record of torture. There was no record of systematic or official military brutality. No priests were ever murdered in Nicaragua. There were in fact three priests in the government, two Jesuits and a Maryknoll missionary. The totalitarian dungeons were actually next door, in El Salvador and Guatemala. The United States had brought down the democratically elected government of Guatemala in 1954 and it is estimated that over 200,000 people had been victims of successive military dictatorships.

Six of the most distinguished Jesuits in the world were viciously murdered at the Central American University in San Salvador in 1989 by a battalion of the Alcatl regiment trained at Fort Benning, Georgia, USA. That extremely brave man Archbishop Romero was assassinated while saying mass. It is estimated that 75,000 people died. Why were they killed? They were killed because they believed a better life was possible and should be achieved. That belief immediately qualified them as communists. They died because they dared to question the status quo, the endless plateau of poverty, disease, degradation and oppression, which had been their birthright.

The United States finally brought down the Sandinista government. It took some years and considerable resistance but relentless economic persecution and 30,000 dead finally undermined the spirit of the Nicaraguan people. They were exhausted and poverty stricken once again. The casinos moved back into the country. Free health and free education were over. Big business returned with a vengeance. 'Democracy' had prevailed.

But this 'policy' was by no means restricted to Central America. It was conducted throughout the world. It was never-ending. And it is as if it never happened.

The United States supported and in many cases engendered every right wing military dictatorship in the world after the end of the Second World War. I refer to Indonesia, Greece, Uruguay, Brazil, Paraguay, Haiti, Turkey, the Philippines, Guatemala, El Salvador, and, of course, Chile. The horror the United States inflicted upon Chile in 1973 can never be purged and can never be forgiven.

Hundreds of thousands of deaths took place throughout these countries. Did they take place? And are they in all cases attributable to US foreign policy? The answer is yes they did take place and they are attributable to American foreign policy. But you wouldn't know it.

It never happened. Nothing ever happened. Even while it was happening it wasn't happening. It didn't matter. It was of no interest. The crimes of the United States have been systematic, constant, vicious, remorseless, but very few people have actually talked about them. You have to hand it to America. It has exercised a quite clinical manipulation of power worldwide while masquerading as a force for universal good. It's a brilliant, even witty, highly successful act of hypnosis.

I put to you that the United States is without doubt the greatest show on the road. Brutal, indifferent, scornful and ruthless it may be but it is also very clever. As a salesman it is out on its own and its most saleable commodity is self love. It's a winner. Listen to all American presidents on television say the words, 'the American people', as in the sentence, 'I say to the American people it is time to pray and to defend the rights of the American people and I ask the American people to trust their president in the action he is about to take on behalf of the American people.'

It's a scintillating stratagem. Language is actually employed to keep thought at bay. The words 'the American people' provide a truly voluptuous cushion of reassurance. You don't need to think. Just lie back on the cushion. The cushion may be suffocating your intelligence and your critical faculties but it's very comfortable. This does not apply of course to the 40 million people living below the poverty line and the 2 million men and women imprisoned in the vast gulag of prisons, which extends across the US.

The United States no longer bothers about low intensity conflict. It no longer sees any point in being reticent or even devious. It puts its cards on the table without fear or favour. It quite simply doesn't give a damn about the United Nations, international law or critical dissent, which it regards as impotent and irrelevant. It also has its own bleating little lamb tagging behind it on a lead, the pathetic and supine Great Britain.

What has happened to our moral sensibility? Did we ever have any? What do these words mean? Do they refer to a term very rarely employed these days – conscience? A conscience to do not only with our own acts but to do with our shared responsibility in the acts of others? Is all this dead? Look at Guantánamo Bay. Hundreds of people detained without charge for over three years, with no legal representation or due process, technically detained forever. This totally illegitimate structure is maintained in defiance of the Geneva Convention. It is not only tolerated but hardly thought about by what's called the 'international community'. This criminal outrage is being committed by a country, which declares itself to be 'the leader of the free world'. Do we think about the inhabitants of Guantánamo Bay? What does the media say about them? They pop up occasionally – a small item on page six. They have been consigned to a no man's land from which indeed they may never return. At present many are on hunger strike, being force-fed, including British residents. No niceties in these force-feeding procedures. No sedative or anaesthetic. Just a tube stuck up your nose and into your throat. You vomit blood. This is torture. What has the British Foreign Secretary said about this? Nothing. What has the British Prime Minister said about this? Nothing. Why not? Because the United States has said: to criticise our conduct in Guantánamo Bay constitutes an unfriendly act. You're either with us or against us. So Blair shuts up.

The invasion of Iraq was a bandit act, an act of blatant state terrorism, demonstrating absolute contempt for the concept of international law. The invasion was an arbitrary military action inspired by a series of lies upon lies and gross manipulation of the media and therefore of the public; an act intended to consolidate American military and economic control of the Middle East masquerading – as a last resort – all other justifications having failed to justify themselves – as liberation. A formidable assertion of military force responsible for the death and mutilation of thousands and thousands of innocent people.

We have brought torture, cluster bombs, depleted uranium, innumerable acts of random murder, misery, degradation and death to the Iraqi people and call it 'bringing freedom and democracy to the Middle East'.

How many people do you have to kill before you qualify to be described as a mass murderer and a war criminal? One hundred thousand? More than enough, I would have thought. Therefore it is just that Bush and Blair be arraigned before the International Criminal Court of Justice. But Bush has been clever. He has not ratified the International Criminal Court of Justice. Therefore if any American soldier or for that matter politician finds himself in the dock Bush has warned that he will send in the marines. But Tony Blair has ratified the Court and is therefore available for prosecution. We can let the Court have his address if they're interested. It is Number 10, Downing Street, London.

Death in this context is irrelevant. Both Bush and Blair place death well away on the back burner. At least 100,000 Iraqis were killed by American bombs and missiles before the Iraq insurgency began. These people are of no moment. Their deaths don't exist. They are blank. They are not even recorded as being dead. 'We don't do body counts,' said the American general Tommy Franks.

Early in the invasion there was a photograph published on the front page of British newspapers of Tony Blair kissing the cheek of a little Iraqi boy. 'A grateful child,' said the caption. A few days later there was a story and photograph, on an inside page, of another four-year-old boy with no arms. His family had been blown up by a missile. He was the only survivor. 'When do I get my arms back?' he asked. The story was dropped. Well, Tony Blair wasn't holding him in his arms, nor the body of any other mutilated child, nor the body of any bloody corpse. Blood is dirty. It dirties your shirt and tie when you're making a sincere speech on television.

The 2,000 American dead are an embarrassment. They are transported to their graves in the dark. Funerals are unobtrusive, out of harm's way. The mutilated rot in their beds, some for the rest of their lives. So the dead and the mutilated both rot, in different kinds of graves.

Here is an extract from a poem by Pablo Neruda, 'I'm Explaining a Few Things':

> *And one morning all that was burning,*
> *one morning the bonfires*
> *leapt out of the earth*
> *devouring human beings*
> *and from then on fire,*
> *gunpowder from then on,*
> *and from then on blood.*
> *Bandits with planes and Moors,*
> *bandits with finger-rings and duchesses,*
> *bandits with black friars spattering blessings*
> *came through the sky to kill children*
> *and the blood of children ran through the streets*
> *without fuss, like children's blood.*
>
> *Jackals that the jackals would despise*
> *stones that the dry thistle would bite on and spit out,*
> *vipers that the vipers would abominate.*
>
> *Face to face with you I have seen the blood*
> *of Spain tower like a tide*
> *to drown you in one wave*
> *of pride and knives.*
>
> *Treacherous*
> *generals:*
> *see my dead house,*
> *look at broken Spain:*
> *from every house burning metal flows*

> *instead of flowers*
> *from every socket of Spain*
> *Spain emerges*
> *and from every dead child a rifle with eyes*
> *and from every crime bullets are born*
> *which will one day find*
> *the bull's eye of your hearts.*
>
> *And you will ask: why doesn't his poetry*
> *speak of dreams and leaves*
> *and the great volcanoes of his native land.*
>
> *Come and see the blood in the streets.*
> *Come and see*
> *the blood in the streets.*
> *Come and see the blood*
> *in the streets!**

Let me make it quite clear that in quoting from Neruda's poem I am in no way comparing Republican Spain to Saddam Hussein's Iraq. I quote Neruda because nowhere in contemporary poetry have I read such a powerful visceral description of the bombing of civilians.

I have said earlier that the United States is now totally frank about putting its cards on the table. That is the case. Its official declared policy is now defined as 'full spectrum dominance'. That is not my term, it is theirs. 'Full spectrum dominance' means control of land, sea, air and space and all attendant resources.

The United States now occupies 702 military installations throughout the world in 132 countries, with the honourable exception of Sweden, of course. We don't quite know how they got there but they are there all right.

The United States possesses 8,000 active and operational nuclear warheads. Two thousand are on hair trigger alert, ready to be launched with 15 minutes warning. It is developing new systems of nuclear force, known as bunker busters. The British, ever cooperative, are intending to replace their own nuclear missile, Trident. Who, I wonder, are they aiming at? Osama bin Laden? You? Me? Joe Dokes? China? Paris? Who knows? What we do know is that this infantile insanity – the possession and threatened use of nuclear weapons – is at the heart of present American political philosophy. We must remind ourselves that the United States is on a permanent military footing and shows no sign of relaxing it.

Many thousands, if not millions, of people in the United States itself are demonstrably sickened, shamed and angered by their government's actions, but as things stand they are not a coherent political force – yet. But the anxiety, uncertainty and fear which we can see growing daily in the United States is unlikely to diminish.

I know that President Bush has many extremely competent speech writers but

I would like to volunteer for the job myself. I propose the following short address which he can make on television to the nation. I see him grave, hair carefully combed, serious, winning, sincere, often beguiling, sometimes employing a wry smile, curiously attractive, a man's man.

'God is good. God is great. God is good. My God is good. Bin Laden's God is bad. His is a bad God. Saddam's God was bad, except he didn't have one. He was a barbarian. We are not barbarians. We don't chop people's heads off. We believe in freedom. So does God. I am not a barbarian. I am the democratically elected leader of a freedom-loving democracy. We are a compassionate society. We give compassionate electrocution and compassionate lethal injection. We are a great nation. I am not a dictator. He is. I am not a barbarian. He is. And he is. They all are. I possess moral authority. You see this fist? This is my moral authority. And don't you forget it.'

A writer's life is a highly vulnerable, almost naked activity. We don't have to weep about that. The writer makes his choice and is stuck with it. But it is true to say that you are open to all the winds, some of them icy indeed. You are out on your own, out on a limb. You find no shelter, no protection – unless you lie – in which case of course you have constructed your own protection and, it could be argued, become a politician.

I have referred to death quite a few times this evening. I shall now quote a poem of my own called 'Death'.

Where was the dead body found?
Who found the dead body?
Was the dead body dead when found?
How was the dead body found?

Who was the dead body?

Who was the father or daughter or brother
Or uncle or sister or mother or son
Of the dead and abandoned body?

Was the body dead when abandoned?
Was the body abandoned?
By whom had it been abandoned?

Was the dead body naked or dressed for a journey?

What made you declare the dead body dead?
Did you declare the dead body dead?
How well did you know the dead body?
How did you know the dead body was dead?

Did you wash the dead body
Did you close both its eyes
Did you bury the body
Did you leave it abandoned
Did you kiss the dead body

When we look into a mirror we think the image that confronts us is accurate. But move a millimetre and the image changes. We are actually looking at a never-ending range of reflections. But sometimes a writer has to smash the mirror – for it is on the other side of that mirror that the truth stares at us.

I believe that despite the enormous odds which exist, unflinching, unswerving, fierce intellectual determination, as citizens, to define the *real* truth of our lives and our societies is a crucial obligation which devolves upon us all. It is in fact mandatory.

If such a determination is not embodied in our political vision we have no hope of restoring what is so nearly lost to us – the dignity of man.

* Extract from 'I'm Explaining a Few Things' translated by Nathaniel Tarn, from Pablo Neruda: *Selected Poems*, published by Jonathan Cape, London 1970. Used by permission of The Random House Group Limited.

© The Nobel Foundation 2005

Every year thousands of Colombian civilians are murdered by the Colombian army for peacefully opposing the Colombian regime

Join the campaign to support Colombian civil society in their efforts to stop UK military aid to the Colombian army

Justice for Colombia

Help us stop the bloodshed

www.justiceforcolombia.org

Contact JFC: 9 Arkwright Road, London NW3 6AB, Tel. 020 7794 3644

Extraordinary Rendition

Ken Coates

Ken Coates is editor of The Spokesman. *Reviews of his recent book,* Empire No More!, *by Tony Benn, Bruce Kent, Jim Mortimer and others can be read online (at www.spokesmanbooks.com).*

'What I want to do, and this is something that has to be discussed very closely with the Muslim community… is to be in a position where if someone is a foreign national coming to preach in this country, they are not going to be preaching this type of extremism, and if they do, they have just got to understand they're not going to come in. What I am trying to do here is, and this will be followed up with the action in the next few weeks as I think you will see, is to send a clear signal out that the rules of the game have changed.'

Tony Blair, Press Conference, 5th August 2005

'Unless we start to believe in conspiracy theories and that the officials are lying, I am lying and that behind this there is some kind of secret state in league with some dark forces in the US, and we believe Secretary Rice is lying, there is simply no truth in claims that the UK has been involved in rendition.'

Jack Straw speaking to the Foreign Affairs Committee of the House of Commons on 13th December 2005

'The rules of the game have changed.' Tony Blair's press conference on the 5th August 2005 was followed by a whole series of public announcements to the same effect. But precision was nowhere to be found. Which rules have changed, in what game? By whom have the changes been made, and where are they codified? Such systematic vagueness may be appropriate to a threat, but not to a law.

On the 15th August Mr. Blair announced the strengthening of the powers of the Home Office 'to deport those fostering hatred, advocating violence to further their beliefs or justifying or validating such violence.' The Foreign Office, not to be left on the shelf, 'was drawing up a list of websites, bookshops, networks and organisations of people considered to be inciting hatred'. Here the law was about to be invoked, but with similar imprecision. Sin is firmly declared to be sinful, but its boundaries are nowhere delineated. Instead, Mr. Blair said, 'Active engagement with any of this' (whatever it is) 'will be a trigger' for deportation.

All these measures raised an immediate problem in the shape of the European Convention on Human Rights, which forbids deportations to countries that practise torture, even in cases where the pressures of sin might be expected. Mr. Blair had prepared his answer to this objection: special agreements would be negotiated with the torturers not to deploy their skills on those who were about to be forcibly returned to them. There was an immediate chorus of disbelief from human rights organisations, who realistically pointed out that all such undertakings were beyond credibility. Most torturers deny their activities, but to extract such a pledge, leave alone to verify its performance, would test the skills of even the most accomplished diplomats in the British Foreign Services. And such diplomats, judging by the activities of the Foreign Office in and around Iraq, are not so very numerous as might have been desired.

In any case, following on this declaration in August, only one torturing Government, that of Jordan, has in the succeeding months offered to sign up to such an accord. The other torturers, and their name is legion, are too modest to claim credit for their achievements, and quite unwilling to enter into the desired recognizances in future.

But we are bound to admit that the deportation of Mr. Blair's new category of thought criminals covers only the most modest part of the torture industry. We have seen the exposure of the regime in the American prison at Guantánamo, even though extensive measures have been taken to avoid undesirable publicity there. Then there has been the echoing atrocity of behaviour in Abu Ghraib. Macabre revelations have taken their time to percolate through from impromptu dungeons in Afghanistan. And then, in the concluding days of 2005, there has been a welter of accusations about rendition and extraordinary rendition, around the world by a fleet of special CIA planes.

The purposes of these processes vary. Where they result in direct torture of the victims, this is alleged to serve the interests of 'intelligence'. But information gathered from the victims of torture can be in the highest degree unreliable, and certainly some part of the imbecility of the intelligence services in the advanced countries during the prelude to the war in Iraq can be attributed to misinformation gathered by means of torture. An ancillary purpose of this form of intimidation has been to gather evidence in order to secure convictions in the Courts. In Britain, the Law Lords have given their own view on this disreputable activity. Such evidence they have declared to be null.

This most recent disquiet about the torturers began with rather modest revelations. *The New York Times* reported on the deaths (at Bagram in 2002) of two Afghan prisoners.

> 'The prisoner, a slight, 22-year-old taxi driver known only as Dilawar, was hauled from his cell at the detention centre in Bagram, Afghanistan, at around 2 a.m. to answer questions about a rocket attack on an American base. When he arrived in the interrogation room, an interpreter who was present said his legs were bouncing uncontrollably in the plastic chair and his hands were numb. He had been chained by the wrists to the top of his cell for much of the previous four days.
>
> Mr. Dilawar asked for a drink of water, and one of the two interrogators, Specialist Joshua R. Claus, 21, picked up a large plastic bottle. But first he punched a hole in the

bottom, the interpreter said, so as the prisoner fumbled weakly with the cap, the water poured out over his orange prison scrubs. The soldier then grabbed the bottle back and began squirting the water forcefully into Mr. Dilawar's face.

"Come on, drink!" the interpreter said Specialist Claus had shouted, as the prisoner gagged on the spray. "Drink!"

At the interrogators' behest, a guard tried to force the young man to his knees. But his legs, which had been pummelled by the guards for several days, could no longer bend. An interrogator told Mr. Dilawar that he could see a doctor after they finished with him. When he was finally sent back to his cell, though, the guards were instructed only to chain the prisoner back to the ceiling.

"Leave him up," one of the guards quoted Specialist Claus as saying.

Several hours passed before an emergency room doctor finally saw Mr. Dilawar. By then he was dead, his body beginning to stiffen. It would be many months before Army investigators learned a final horrific detail: most of the interrogators had believed Mr. Dilawar was an innocent man who simply drove his taxi past the American base at the wrong time.'

President Hamid Karzai addressed this question in May 2005 when he demanded 'very, very strong action' against abuse by American military personnel. 'The people of the United States are very kind people', he said. 'It is only one or two individuals who are bad.'

There have turned out to be rather more bad individuals than the President suspected. Perhaps his confinement in the secure zone of Kabul has restricted his vision. In fact, since 2001, the Central Intelligence Agency has captured some three thousand people who have been ferried around the world in a fleet of special planes, to be 'rendered'.

According to *Der Spiegel,* there have been 437 CIA flights which have either landed in Germany or crossed German air space. The French are aware of two jets which carried prisoners to Guantánamo. In Britain, 210 flights are alleged to have used British airports. And in Portugal there have been reported 34 such landings. Ten CIA flights are alleged to have touched down at Tenerife and Majorca, whilst 67 flights have, it is claimed, landed in Iceland since the year 2001. In Italy there have been 17 secret flights by the CIA which landed there between July 2002 and May 2005, if we are to believe *Corriere della Sera.*

Plane spotters have been monitoring some of this bizarre tourist trade. Their web pages have listed some of the movements of the flights of a Gulfstream V, one of the CIA's planes, which is recorded as having landed at Jakarta's military airport and taken away Muhammad Saad Iqbal Madni, suspected of working for al Qaeda, to interrogation in Egypt. The plane spotters' lists track the Gulfstream V to Islamabad, Karachi, Riyadh in Saudi Arabia, Dubai, Tashkent in Uzbekistan, Baghdad, Kuwait City, Baku in Azerbaijan, and Rabat in Morocco. The same plane has landed often at Dulles International Airport in the United States, at Jordan's military airport in Amman, and at airports in Frankfurt, Glasgow and Larnaca.

The Guardian reported on December 10th on the activities of Paul, who has been monitoring movements at Glasgow Airport, but who has been in regular contact, they say, with people as far away as Bournemouth and Karachi, building up a picture of this hyperactive network of renditions. One of these volunteers is apparently a Spanish town planner 'who is part of a small group who gather with their long lenses and foil-wrapped sandwiches at Majorca's Son Sant Joan Airport'.

Of course, the very extensive movements that have been monitored in parts of the press do appear to involve rigorous intelligence, and we are bound to wonder whether the volunteer plane spotters may, unbeknown to themselves, have been able to draw upon information volunteered by rogue intelligence specialists. So profound is the alienation engendered by the war in Iraq and its related operations that nobody can be absolutely sure who works for whom in the present heaving spook stew.

Who are the involuntary tourists ferried about by the Central Intelligence Agency? Many of them, perhaps most of them, may have been to some extent involved in terrorism. But others are simply unfortunate victims of error, like the poor taxi driver who was put to death by his interrogators in Bagram. Since this has become a thriving industry, the numbers of innocent victims have, of course, increased.

But there is another victim. Whoever, and however many of the abducted persons are 'wrongly' taken, the kidnap of even the wickedest and most brutal of terrorists strikes a fearsome blow at the rule of law itself.

Henry Porter captures the horror of this situation in a report in *The Observer* on the 11th December 2005.

> 'I heard a story about five Egyptian al Qaeda suspects being arrested in Albania and flown to Egypt. The important part was that this had happened before 11 September 2001 – during the Clinton administration – proof that rendition was an established CIA practice.
>
> So I flew to Tirana, stayed in the Rogner Hotel and waited for various contacts I had been given to return my calls. If you hang about in the Rogner sooner or later you meet everyone you need and with the help of a fixer – one of the few Albanian males I met who was not suffering some mild psychotic disorder – I got to the bottom of the story of how five men were trapped by the electronic surveillance of the local intelligence service and were transported to Cairo by the CIA. They were all tortured and two were hanged.
>
> Since it had all happened in 1998 people didn't mind talking about it. Only when I asked about current operations against al Qaeda in the Balkans did the shutters come down. I left Tirana for Cairo and after many false trails found the facilities where these things were likely to have happened. I also learned that American intelligence officers were part of the process. They did not simply leave the rendered suspects, but remained on hand to receive information produced by the interrogation. That America was collaborating with torturers was shocking, but it was seeing these facilities that brought home to me the terror and despair of the men who were wrung dry before being executed.'

The extent of rendition was convincingly summarised by the Centre for Human Rights and Global Justice in New York University School of Law at the beginning of December 2005. Their findings have been distributed by the All Party Parliamentary Group on Extraordinary Rendition, in the British House of Commons.

> 'Extraordinary Renditions have been widely reported in the media. These public sources indicate, for example, that:
>
> **Ahmed Agiza** and **Mohammed al-Zari** were expelled from Sweden on December 18, 2001, and transferred to Egypt. According to the Swedish TV programme *Kalla Fakta*, both men were flown on a Gulfstream V jet alleged to be owned by a US

company and which reportedly is used mainly by the US Government. The Swedish Government relied upon "diplomatic assurances" from Egypt that the two men would not be tortured and would have fair trials upon return. US agents were involved in the transfer of Agiza and al-Zari. The UN Committee against Torture recently held that in deporting Agiza and al-Zari to Egypt, Sweden violated the *Convention against Torture and Other Cruel, Inhuman or Degrading Treatment or Punishment*.

Egyptian-born **Hassan Osama Nasr** (also known as Abu Omar*) disappeared from his city of residence, Milan, in February 2003. He briefly surfaced fifteen months later, when he called his family in Italy claiming to have been kidnapped by US and Italian forces, taken to Egypt and tortured. Based on the latest available information, Abu Omar is being held in the Tora prison on the edge of the Egyptian capital Cairo. Italian authorities are currently conducting an inquiry into Nasr's purported kidnapping. On 23 June 2005, an Italian judge issued arrest warrants for thirteen alleged CIA agents in connection with Abu Omar's kidnapping. On the same day, another Italian judge issued an indictment against Abu Omar for crimes relating to terrorism. In July 2005, the Italian authorities issued warrants for six more alleged CIA agents accused of helping plan the kidnapping. In November 2005, prosecutors requested that the Italy's Justice Ministry seek the extradition of the CIA agents from the United States.

Khaled El-Masri*, a German citizen born in Lebanon, was arrested by police at the Macedonian border on 21 December 2003. He was then reportedly held in a Macedonian hotel room for twenty-three days. During this time he says he was constantly interrogated by Macedonian agents about connections to Islamic organisations, and accused of having been in a terrorist training camp in Jalalabad. At the end of this time he was allegedly beaten, stripped, shackled, blindfolded, and placed aboard a plane. El-Masri was delivered to a prison in Afghanistan that he says was nominally run by Afghan officials but was actually under US control. While in the prison he was repeatedly interrogated, and photographed naked by individuals el-Masri identified as US agents. US authorities have neither confirmed nor denied these allegations. In May of 2004, el-Masri was returned to Europe, having never been charged with a crime. A reporter, Stephen Grey and the ZDF television show *Frontal 21*, have independently determined that the details of al-Masri's statement coincide with the flight schedule of a US-chartered Boeing 737 used by the CIA. El-Masri's release was reportedly personally ordered by the US Secretary of State Rice after she learned the man had been mistakenly identified as a terrorist suspect. German authorities are currently investigating the case, and have determined that he was in Afghanistan during the time of his disappearance by using isotope analysis of his hair.

In October 2001, **Jamil Qasim Aseed Mohammed**, a Yemeni microbiology student, was allegedly flown from Pakistan to Jordan on a US-registered Gulfstream jet after Pakistan's intelligence agency reportedly surrendered him to US authorities at Karachi airport. US officials alleged that Aseed Mohammed was an al Qaeda operative who played a role in the bombing of the USS *Cole*. The handover of the shackled and blindfolded Aseem Mohammed reportedly took place in the middle of the night in a remote corner of the airport, without the benefit of extradition or deportation procedures.

Apparently acting on information provided by the CIA, Indonesian authorities reportedly detained **Muhammad Saad Iqbal Madni** in early January 2002. Iqbal Madni is suspected by the CIA of having worked with Richard Reid (the "shoe-bomber"). According to a senior Indonesian official, a few days later, Egypt formally asked Indonesia to extradite Iqbal, who carried an Egyptian as well as a Pakistani passport. The request did not specify the crime, noting broadly that Egypt sought Iqbal in connection with terrorism. On 11 January, allegedly without a court hearing or a lawyer, Iqbal was put aboard an unmarked US-registered Gulfstream V jet and flown to Egypt. A senior Indonesian official said that an extradition request from Egypt provided political cover to comply with the CIA's request. "This was a US deal all along", the senior official said, "Egypt just provided the formalities".

In September 2002, US immigration authorities, reportedly with the approval of then-acting Attorney General Larry Thompson, authorised the "expedited removal" of a Syrian-born Canadian citizen, **Maher Arar***, to Syria under section 235(c) of the *Immigration and Nationality Act 1952*. US authorities alleged that Arar had links to al Qaeda. While in transit at John F. Kennedy International Airport in New York, Arar was taken into custody by officials from the FBI and Immigration and Naturalisation Service (since reorganised into the Department of Homeland Security) and shackled. Arar's requests for a lawyer were dismissed on the basis that he was not a US citizen and therefore he did not have the right to counsel. Despite the fact that he is a Canadian citizen and has resided in Canada for seventeen years, Arar's pleas to return to Canada were ignored. Officials repeatedly questioned Arar about his connection to certain members of al Qaeda. Arar denied that he had any connections whatsoever to the named individuals. He was eventually put on a small jet that first landed in Washington DC, and then in Amman, Jordan. Once in Amman, Arar was allegedly blindfolded, shackled and transferred to Syria in a van. Arar was then placed in a prison where he was allegedly beaten for several hours and forced to falsely confess that he had attended a training camp in Afghanistan in order to fight against the US. Arar remained in Syria for ten months during which he was repeatedly beaten, tortured, and kept in a shallow grave. Arar has subsequently been released and returned to Canada. No charges were ever filed against him in any of the countries involved in his transfer. Following intense public pressure, Canada initiated a public inquiry into the circumstances surrounding Arar's transfer. The US has refused the invitation to participate in the Canadian inquiry. US officials, speaking on condition of anonymity, have said that the Arar case fits the profile of extraordinary rendition.

Australian citizen **Mamdouh Habib** was arrested in Pakistan in October 2002 and, reportedly at the request of the US authorities, flown to Egypt where he was allegedly severely tortured. Habib remained in Egypt for six months, after which he was transferred to Guantánamo. On 11 January 2005, Habib was released from Guantánamo without charge and subsequently transferred to Australia.'

Some of these cases we have marked with an asterisk, because they are treated in greater depth below. They have been chosen to exemplify some particular features which are worthy of note, and stand out from the general, very dismal, picture.

At the time of writing, various national Parliaments and the European Parliament have become seized of this question. There are continuing contentious investigations. Allegations have been made that former Soviet air bases in Poland have been taken over by the CIA, and used, alongside similar facilities in Romania, to keep 'senior al Qaeda suspects'. Human Rights Watch reported that some twenty-five prisoners were being held secretly at two bases in Poland, and the American Network ABC quoted CIA sources to say that these prisoners had recently been cleared away from Europe and moved to North Africa, 'to avoid embarrassment during Condoleezza Rice's trip to Europe'.

Meantime, Dick Marty, representing the Council of Europe, has opened an investigation in Poland and elsewhere to ascertain whether or not the Poles' strenuous denials hold water or not.

Alvaro Gil Robles, the Human Rights Commissioner of the Council of Europe, has also come across a questionable installation at the American Camp Bondsteel near Pristina in Kosovo.

Denials, claims and counter-claims darken the air and fill the press with confusing headlines. But the scandal of rendition will not go away, and already there are signs that those politicians who seek to obscure the truth about what has been happening have now passed the point at which their protestations do more damage to their own reputation than they do to the unfortunate victims whose systematic mistreatment has darkened the earliest days of the twenty-first century.

Those who are concerned to treasure human rights, and build a culture of freedom, are already reaching the point of no return, and will soon be recognising a new need: that we must start again to build a society and a polity where men and women can breathe freely.

Renditions – Does Europe collaborate with US?

There has been an informal agreement between the European Union and the United States that flights to and from the US can stop-over in transit at EU airports since around 1998. The US requested these 'facilities' into order to send people back to Africa, the Middle East and Asia. No figures have ever been published on the extent to which this agreement has been used.

A year after the invasion of Iraq, the minutes of a high-level meeting entitled 'New Transatlantic Agenda: EU-US meeting on Justice and Home Affairs', in Athens on 22 January 2003, record that:

> 'Both sides agreed on... increased use of European transit facilities to support the return of criminal/inadmissible aliens'

The official minutes of the meeting on the public register of the Council of the European Union (the 25 governments) is only 'partially accessible' – that is to say that all the details concerning the US have been deleted (censored). A spokesperson for the Council said the deletions were a *'courtesy'* to the USA.

The European Commission claim that EU transit facilities were only used for failed asylum-seekers and illegal immigrants, 'not rendition' of CIA suspects. But the minutes of the Athens meeting refer to the return of *'criminal/inadmissible aliens'*. Who are the 'criminals'? Are they convicted or suspected? What crimes have they committed, or are they suspected of committing? Who are the inadmissible aliens, where are they being returned to, and under what physical conditions?

Tony Bunyan, Statewatch editor, comments:

> 'Whether these US transit flights are for "criminals", "inadmissible aliens" or for rendition, the same questions arise.
>
> Do EU governments know how many times their airports have been used for "transit" by US government flights? Which airports are used? How many people have been moved in this way? How many "criminals" and how many "inadmissible aliens"? If they do, then why are the facts and figures not available? And if they do not know, why not?
>
> If EU governments do not know who is being moved and where by foreign agencies using their airports then they are grossly irresponsible. To "aid and abet" the movement of people in an inhuman or degrading way, or to be tortured, is a crime.'

Source: www.statewatch.org, 15 December 2005

Extraordinary Rendition
Case Study I

Maher Arar's story

Maher Arar was born in Syria. He came to Canada with his family when he was seventeen years old, and became a Canadian citizen in 1991.

On 26 September 2002, while in transit at New York's John F Kennedy Airport, he was detained by US officials and interrogated about alleged links to al Qaeda. Twelve days later, he was chained, shackled and flown to Jordan aboard a private plane and from there transferred to a Syrian prison. In Syria, he was held in a tiny 'grave-like' cell for ten months and ten days before he was moved to a different prison. He was beaten, tortured and forced to make a false confession.

On 28 January 2004, the Canadian Government announced a Commission of Inquiry into the Actions of Canadian officials in relation to Maher Arar.

This is Mr Arar's statement to the media on 4 November 2003.

There have been many allegations made about me in the media, all of them by people who refuse to be named or come forward. So before I tell you who I am and what happened to me, I will tell you who I am not.

I am not a terrorist. I am not a member of al Qaeda and I do not know any one who belongs to this group. All I know about al Qaeda is what I have seen in the media. I have never been to Afghanistan. I have never been anywhere near Afghanistan, and I do not have any desire ever to go to Afghanistan.

Now, let me tell you who I am.

I am a Syrian-born Canadian. I moved here with my parents when I was seventeen years old. I went to university and studied hard, and eventually obtained a Masters degree in telecommunications. I met my wife, Monia, at McGill University. We fell in love and eventually married in 1994. I knew then that she was special, but I had no idea how special she would turn out to be.

If it were not for her I believe I would still be in prison.

We had our first child, a daughter named Barâa, in February 1997. She is six years old now. In December 1997, we moved to Ottawa from Montreal. I took a job with a high tech firm, called The MathWorks, in Boston in 1999, and my job involved a lot of travel within the United States.

Then, in 2001, I decided to come back to Ottawa to start my own consulting company. We had our second child, Houd, in February 2002. He is twenty months old now.

So this is who I am. I am a father and a husband. I am a telecommunications engineer and entrepreneur. I have never had trouble with the police, and have always been a good citizen. So I still cannot believe what has happened to me, and how my life and career have been destroyed.

In September 2002, I was with my wife and children, and her family, vacationing in Tunis. I got an email from MathWorks saying that they might need me soon to assess potential consulting work for one of their customers. I said goodbye to my wife and family, and headed back home to prepare for work.

I was using my air-miles to travel, and the best flight I could get went from Tunis, to Zurich, to New York, to Montreal. My flight arrived in New York at 2pm on September 26th 2002. I had a few hours to wait until my connecting flight to Montreal.

This is when my nightmare began. I was pulled aside at immigration and taken to another area. Two hours later, some officials came and told me this was regular procedure and they took my fingerprints and photographs.

Then some police came and searched my bags and copied my Canadian passport. I was getting worried, and I asked what was going on, and they would not answer. I asked to make a phone call, and they would not let me.

Then a team of people came and told me they wanted to ask me some questions. One man was from the Federal Bureau of Investigation (FBI), and another was from the New York Police Department. I was scared and did not know what was going on. I told them I wanted a lawyer. They told me I had no right to a lawyer, because I was not an American citizen.

They asked me where I worked and how much money I made. They swore at me, and insulted me. It was very humiliating. They wanted me to answer every question quickly. They were consulting a report while they were questioning me, and the information they had was so private, I thought this must be from Canada.

I told them everything I knew. They asked me about my travel in the United States. I told them about my work permits, and my business there. They asked about information on my computer and whether I was willing to share it. I welcomed the idea, but I don't know if they did.

They asked me about different people, some I know, and most I do not. They asked me about Abdullah Almalki, and I told them I worked with his brother at high tech firms in Ottawa, and that the Almalki family had come from Syria about the same time as mine. I told them I did not know Abdullah well, but had seen him a few times and I described the times I could remember. I told them I had a casual relationship with him.

They were so rude with me, yelling at me that I had a selective memory.

Then they pulled out a copy of my rental lease from 1997. I could not believe they had this. I was completely shocked. They pointed out that Abdullah had signed the lease as a witness. I had completely forgotten that he had signed it for me. When we moved to Ottawa in 1997, we needed someone to witness our lease, and I phoned Abdullah's brother, and he could not come, so he sent Abdullah.

But they thought I was hiding this. I told them the truth. I had nothing to hide. I had never had problems in the United States before, and I could not believe what was happening to me.

This interrogation continued until midnight. I was very, very worried, and asked for a lawyer again and again. They just ignored me. Then they put me in chains, on my wrists and ankles, and took me in a van to a place where many people were being held at another building by the airport. They would not tell me what was happening.

At one in the morning they put me in a room with metal benches in it. I could not sleep. I was very, very scared and disoriented. The next morning they started questioning me again. They asked me about what I think about Bin Laden, Palestine, Iraq. They also asked me about the mosques I pray in, my bank accounts, my e-mail addresses, my relatives, about everything.

This continued on and off for eight hours.

Then a man from the Immigration and Naturalisation Service came in and told me they wanted me to volunteer to go to Syria. I said no way. I said I wanted to go home to Canada or sent back to Switzerland. He said to me 'you are a special interest'.

They asked me to sign a form. They would not let me read it, but I just signed it. I was exhausted and confused and disoriented. I had not slept or eaten since I was in the plane.

At about six in the evening they brought me a cold McDonalds meal to eat. This was the first food I had eaten since the last meal I had on the plane.

At about eight o'clock they put all the shackles and chains back on, and put me in a van, and drove me to a prison. I later learned this was the Metropolitan Detention Centre. They would not tell me what was happening, or where I was going.

They strip-searched me. It was humiliating. They put me in an orange suit, and took me to a doctor, where they made me sign forms, and gave me a vaccination. I asked what it was, and they would not tell me. My arm was red for almost two weeks from that.

They took me to a cell. I had never seen a prison before in my life, and I was terrified. I asked again for a phone call, and a lawyer. They just ignored me. They treated me differently to the other prisoners. They would not give me a toothbrush or toothpaste, or reading material. I did get a copy of the Koran about two days later.

After five days, they let me make a phone call. I called Monia's mother, who was here in Ottawa, and told her I was scared they might send me to Syria, and asked her to help find me a lawyer. They would only let me talk for two minutes.

On the seventh or eighth day they brought me a document, saying they had decided to deport me, and I had a choice of where to be deported. I wrote that I wanted to go to Canada. It asked if I had concerns about going to Canada. I wrote no, and signed it.

The Canadian consul came on October 4, and I told her I was scared of being deported to Syria. She told me that would not happen. She told me that a lawyer was being arranged. I was very upset, and scared. I could barely talk.

The next day, a lawyer came. She told me not to sign any document unless she was present. We could only talk for 30 minutes. She said she would try to help me. That was a Saturday.

On Sunday night at about 9pm, the guards came to my cell and told me my lawyer was there to see me. I thought it was a strange time, and they took me into a room with seven or eight people in it. I asked where my lawyer was. They told me he had refused to come and started questioning me again. They said they wanted to know why I did not want to go back to Syria. I told them I would be tortured there. I told them I had not done my military service; I am a Sunni Muslim; my mother's cousin had been accused of being a member of the Muslim Brotherhood and was put in prison for nine years.

They asked me to sign a document and I refused. I told them they could not send me to Syria. I would be tortured. I asked again for a lawyer. At three in the morning they took me back to my cell.

At three in the morning on Tuesday, October 8, a prison guard woke me up and told me I was leaving. They took me to another room and stripped and searched me again. Then they again chained and shackled me. Then two officials took me inside a room and read me what they said was a decision by the Immigration Director.

They told me that, based on classified information that they could not reveal to me, I would be deported to Syria. I said again that I would be tortured there. Then they read part of the document where it explained that the Immigration Service was not the body that deals with the Geneva Convention regarding torture.

Then they took me outside into a car and drove me to an airport in New Jersey. They put me on a small private jet. I was the only person on the plane with them. I was still chained and shackled. We flew first to Washington. A new team of people got on the plane and the others left. I overheard them talking on the phone, saying that Syria was refusing to take me directly, but Jordan would take me.

Then we flew to Portland, to Rome, and then to Amman, Jordan. All the time I was on the plane I was thinking how to avoid being tortured. I was very scared. We landed in Amman at three in the morning local time on October 9.

They took me out of plane and there were six or seven Jordanian men waiting for us. They blindfolded and chained me, and put me in a van.

They made me bend my head down in the back seat. Then, these men started beating me. Every time I tried to talk they beat me. For the first few minutes it was very intense.

Thirty minutes later we arrived at a building where they took off my blindfold and asked routine questions, before taking me to a cell. It was around 4:30 in the morning on October 9. Later that day, they took my fingerprints, and blindfolded me and put me in a van. I asked where I was going, and they told me I was going back to Montreal.

About forty-five minutes later, I was put into a different car. These men started beating me again. They made me keep my head down, and it was very uncomfortable, but every time I moved, they beat me again. Over an hour later we arrived at what I think was the border with Syria. I was put in another car and we drove for another three hours.

I was taken into a building, where some guards went through my bags and took some chocolates I bought in Zurich. I asked one of the people where I was and he told me I was in the Palestine branch of the Syrian military intelligence. It was now about six in the evening on October 9.

Three men came and took me into a room. I was very, very scared. They put me on a chair, and one of the men started asking me questions. I later learned this man was a colonel. He asked me about my brothers, and why we had left Syria. I answered all the questions.

If I did not answer quickly enough, he would point to a metal chair in the corner and ask 'Do you want me to use this?' I did not know then what that chair was for. I learned later it was used to torture people.

I asked him what he wanted to hear. I was terrified, and I did not want to be tortured. I would say anything to avoid torture. This lasted for four hours. There was no violence, only threats this day. At about one in the morning, the guards came to take me to my cell downstairs.

We went into the basement, and they opened a door, and I looked in. I could not believe what I saw. I asked how long I would be kept in this place. He did not answer, but put me in and closed the door. It was like a grave. It had no light. It was three feet wide. It was six feet deep. It was seven feet high. It had a metal door, with a small opening in the door, which did not let in light because there was a piece of metal on the outside for sliding things into the cell.

There was a small opening in the ceiling, about one foot by two feet with iron bars. Over that was another ceiling, so only a little light came through this. There were cats and rats up there, and from time to time the cats peed through the opening into the cell. There were two blankets, two dishes and two bottles. One bottle was for water and the other one was used for urinating during the night. Nothing else. No light.

I spent ten months and ten days inside that grave.

The next day I was taken upstairs again. The beating started that day and was very intense for a week, and then less intense for another week. The second and the third days were the worst. I could hear other prisoners being tortured, and screaming and screaming. Interrogations are carried out in different rooms.

One tactic they use is to question prisoners for two hours, and then put them in a waiting room, so they can hear the others screaming, and then bring them back to continue the interrogation.

The cable is a black electrical cable, about two inches thick. They hit me with it everywhere on my body. They mostly aimed for my palms, but sometimes missed and hit my wrists. They were sore and red for three weeks. They also struck me on my hips, and lower back. Interrogators constantly threatened me with the metal chair, tyre and electric shocks.

The tyre is used to restrain prisoners while they torture them with beating on the soles of their feet. I guess I was lucky, because they put me in the tyre, but only as a threat. I was not beaten while in the tyre.

They used the cable on the second and third day, and after that mostly beat me with their hands, hitting me in the stomach and on the back of my neck, and slapping me on the face. Where they hit me with the cables, my skin turned blue for two or three weeks, but there was no bleeding. At the end of the day they told me tomorrow would be worse. So I could not sleep.

Then, on the third day, the interrogation lasted about eighteen hours.

They beat me from time to time and made me wait in the waiting room for one to two hours before resuming the interrogation. While in the waiting room I heard a lot of people screaming. They wanted me to say I went to Afghanistan. This was a surprise to me. They had not asked about this in the United States.

They kept beating me so I had to falsely confess and told them I did go to Afghanistan. I was ready to confess to anything if it would stop the torture. They wanted me to say I went to a training camp. I was so scared I urinated on myself twice. The beating was less severe each of the following days.

At the end of each day, they would always say, 'Tomorrow will be harder for you.' So each night, I could not sleep – I did not sleep for the first four days, and slept no more than two hours a day for about two months. Most of the time I was not taken back to my cell, but to the waiting room where I could hear all the prisoners being tortured and screaming.

One time, I heard them banging a man's head repeatedly on a desk really hard.

Around October 17, the beatings subsided. Their next tactic was to take me in a room, blindfolded, and people would talk about me. I could hear them saying, 'He knows lots of people who are terrorists'; 'We will get their numbers'; 'He is a liar'; 'He has been out of the country for long.' Then they would say, 'Let's be frank, let's be friends, tell us the truth,' and come around the desk, and slap me on the face. They played lots of mind games.

The interrogation and beating ended three days before I had my first consular visit, on October 23. I was taken from my cell and my beard was shaved. I was taken to another building, and there was the colonel in the hallway with some other men and they all seemed very nervous and agitated.

I did not know what was happening and they would not tell me. They never say what is happening. You never know what will happen next. I was told not to tell anything about the beating. Then I was taken into a room for a ten minute meeting with the consul. The colonel was there, and three other Syrian officials including an interpreter. I cried a lot at that meeting. I could not say anything about the torture. I thought if I did, I would not get any more visits, or I might be beaten again.

After that visit, about a month after I arrived, they called me up to sign and place my thumb print on a document about seven pages long. They would not let me read it, but I had to put my thumb print and signature on the bottom of each page. It was handwritten.

Another document was about three pages long, with questions: Who are your friends? How long have you been out of the country? The last question was empty lines. They answered the questions with their own handwriting, except for the last one, where I was forced to write that I had been to Afghanistan.

The consular visits were my lifeline, but I also found them very frustrating. There were seven consular visits, and one visit from members of parliament. After the visits I would bang my head and my fist on the wall in frustration. I needed the visits, but I could not say anything there.

I got new clothes after the December 10th consular visit. Until then, I had been wearing the same clothes since being on the jet from the United States.

On three different occasions in December I had a very hard time. Memories crowded my mind and I thought I was going to lose control, and I just screamed and screamed. I could not breathe well after, and felt very dizzy.

I was not exposed to sunlight for six months. The only times I left the grave was for interrogation, and for the visits. Daily life in that place was hell. When I was detained in New York I weighed about 180 pounds. I think I lost about 40 pounds while I was at the Palestine Branch.

On August 19, I was taken upstairs to see the investigator, and I was given a paper and asked to write what he dictated. If I protested, he kicked me. I was forced to write that I went to a training camp in Afghanistan. They made me sign and put my thumbprint on the last page.

The same day I was transferred to a different place, which I learnt later was the Investigation Branch. I was placed there in a 12 feet by 20 feet collective cell. We were about 50 people in that place.

The next day I was taken to the Sednaya prison. I was very lucky that I was not tortured when I arrived there. All the other prisoners were tortured when they arrived.

Sednaya prison was like heaven for me. I could move around, and talk with other prisoners. I could buy food to eat and I gained a lot of weight there. I was only beaten once there.

On around September 19 or 20, I heard the other prisoners saying that another Canadian had arrived there. I looked up, and saw a man, but I did not recognise him. His head was shaved, and he was very, very thin and pale. He was very weak. When I looked closer, I recognised him. It was Abdullah Almalki. He told me he had also been at the Palestine Branch, and that he had also been in a grave like I had been, except he had been in it longer.

He told me he had been severely tortured with the tyre, and the cable. He was also hanged upside down. He was tortured much worse than me. He had also been tortured when he was brought to Sednaya, so that was only two weeks before.

I do not know why they have Abdullah there. What I can say for sure is that no human deserves to be treated the way he was, and I hope that Canada does all they can to help him.

On September 28 I was taken out and blindfolded and put in what felt like a bus and taken back to the Palestine Branch. They would not tell me what was happening, and I was scared I was going back to the grave. Instead, I was put in one of the waiting rooms where they torture people. I could hear the prisoners being tortured, and screaming, again.

The same day I was called in to an office to answer more questions, about what I would say if I came back to Canada. They did not tell me I would be released. I was put back in the waiting room, and I was kept there for one week, listening to all the prisoners screaming. It was awful.

On Sunday October 5, I was taken out and into a car and driven to a court. I was put in a room with a prosecutor. I asked for a lawyer and he said I did not need one. I asked what was going on and he read from my confession. I tried to argue I was beaten and did not go to Afghanistan, but he did not listen. He did not tell me what I was charged with, but told me to stamp my fingerprint and sign on a document he would not let me see. Then he said I would be released.

Then I was taken back to the Palestine Branch where I met the head of the Syrian Military Intelligence and officials from the Canadian Embassy. And then I was released.

I want to conclude by thanking all of the people who worked for my release, especially my wife Monia, and human rights groups, and all the people who wrote letters, and all the members of parliament who stood up for justice. Of course, I thank all of the journalists for covering my story.

The past year has been a nightmare, and I have spent the past few weeks at home trying to learn how to live with what happened to me. I know that the only way I will ever be able to move on in my life and have a future is if I can find out why this happened to me.

What is at stake here is the future of our country, the interests of Canadian citizens, and most importantly Canada's international reputation for being a leader in human rights where citizens from different ethnic groups are treated no different than other Canadians.

Extraordinary Rendition Case Study II

Abu Omar's story

Abu Omar, also known as Hassan Osama Nasr, was born in Egypt. He lived in Albania and, reportedly, in Germany, before moving to Italy where he was an imam at a mosque in Milan. In February 2003, he was abducted on the streets of Milan and rendered to Egypt via Germany. He has been imprisoned there ever since, except for a short period of release in 2004. Then, he contacted his wife and others in Italy by phone and told of his abduction by Americans and subsequent torture in Egypt. He was detained again shortly afterwards, and nothing has been heard from him since.

In December 2005, a Milan court issued a European arrest warrant for 22 CIA agents suspected of kidnapping an Egyptian cleric while he was walking in the street in February 2003. Milan magistrates suspect a CIA team grabbed Hassan Mustafa Osama Nasr and flew him for interrogation to Egypt, where he said he was tortured. Justice officials believe Nasr, also known as Abu Omar, is still in custody in Egypt.

In November, prosecutors asked the Italian Justice Ministry to seek the extradition of the suspects from the United States, but Justice Minister Roberto Castelli has not yet decided whether to act on the request.

A European Union warrant is automatically valid across the 25-nation bloc and does not require approval of any government. Prosecutor Armando Spataro told Reuters he had also asked Interpol to try to detain the suspects anywhere in the world.

Italian Prime Minister Silvio Berlusconi said he did not believe CIA agents had kidnapped Nasr, but added that governments were not going to defeat terrorism by playing by the rules.

Following his abduction in 2003, nothing was heard from Abu Omar for more than a year, until he telephoned his family in Italy saying that he had been kidnapped by US forces, taken to Egypt and tortured. His story is long and complex. It has been extensively covered in the *Chicago Tribune* newspaper, which is the source for much of what follows.

Four days before Abu Omar vanished, three American visitors, two men and a woman, checked into the Milan Hilton Hotel. Their passports, visa cards and driving licences appeared genuine enough. But the names on these documents were bogus. So was their shared corporate address, a non-existent company with a post office box in Washington. According to the Italian authorities, the three Americans were members of a larger covert team assigned to snatch Abu Omar off the street and ship him back to Egypt.

Although the CIA refuses to talk about the Milan abduction or even acknowledge that it occurred, documents obtained by the *Chicago Tribune* clearly link the intelligence agency with the identities, addresses and cell phones used by several of the American operatives.

Egyptian Prime Minister Ahmed Nazief, whose country has received more renditions than any other, told a group of *Tribune* reporters and editors that he was aware of '60 or 70' cases in which US agents have seized Egyptian nationals abroad and flown them to Egypt. In most of the known renditions, suspects have been arrested by the local authorities in such countries as Indonesia, Sweden and Macedonia before being handed over to the CIA.

In the case of Abu Omar, the absence of any prior arrest has left the CIA open to kidnapping charges. Indeed, the police in Milan, who had been tapping Abu Omar's telephone, were as surprised as his wife and friends by his sudden disappearance. When they learned he was gone, the police opened a missing-person investigation.

Armando Spataro, the Milan prosecutor who requested the arrest warrants, said the names of those accused were taken from the passports and other documents used at hotels and car rental agencies in Milan. He believed that most of the names were probably not the true identities of the accused kidnappers. But his team have pictures of the suspects taken from photocopies of their passports made by hotels.

'We have a convention for mutual cooperation with the US in criminal matters,' Spataro said. 'I will ask them to identify some people, and I will ask them to interrogate [the suspects], because I don't believe they will surrender them to Italy voluntarily.' Spataro dismissed suggestions that Abu Omar's abductors, who like many CIA officers working abroad may have been posing as American diplomats, might enjoy diplomatic immunity from criminal prosecution. 'If we have evidence of their involvement in kidnapping, there is no immunity for that,' he said.

A senior official with the prosecutor's office, speaking on condition of anonymity, confirmed that one of those accused was a CIA officer posing as a US diplomat in Milan at the time of Abu Omar's abduction. The official said that the diplomat was well known as the CIA's representative in Milan and that the dozen other suspects charged had been in cell phone contact with him during their stay in Milan. The diplomat is believed to have left Italy.

The Italian court also issued a warrant for the arrest of Abu Omar. The 103-page document consists mostly of transcripts of conversations picked up by police wiretaps and microphones before his abduction. Prosecution sources said the warrant was sought principally in the hope of forcing Egypt to return Abu Omar to Milan. The Egyptian government has ignored two formal diplomatic requests, sent last year through the Italian Justice Ministry, asking for confirmation that Abu Omar is in Egypt and an explanation of how and why he entered Egypt.

Spataro also is seeking permission to interview Abu Omar's mother, his two brothers, his sister and a prominent lawyer, all of whom are believed to be living in the Egyptian port city of Alexandria. 'We asked the Egyptian authorities for their cooperation, but they haven't responded,' Spataro said.

Judging from the information gleaned by Spataro's investigators, the abduction of Abu Omar on the afternoon of 17 February 2003 was an elaborate and expensive operation. The 18 people brought into the city for the operation spent at least $150,000 at the Marriott, Hilton, Sheraton and Westin hotels, according to documents obtained by the *Chicago Tribune*. Nearly all gave post office boxes as their home or business addresses. Those names and addresses are linked to what appears to be a CIA network of dozens of post office boxes in the Washington area with hundreds of names attached.

Hotel records show that several of the 13 suspects visited Milan in early January and then left, suggesting that the abduction operation was put on hold at the beginning of 2003. The first to return, on 1 February 2003, was a 33-year-old woman with a Hispanic-sounding name whose passport said she was a native of Florida. She was joined two days later by six other alleged team members and five more the day after that. They included a 64-year-old man whose passport said he had been born in Alaska, a 57-year-old woman whose passport said she had been born in Florida, and a 50-year-old man whose US passport said he had been born in the former Soviet republic of Moldova.

The Moldovan-born man listed his US employer's address as a post office box in Arlington, Virginia, across the Potomac River from Washington. His name is linked, via a half-dozen post office boxes in the Washington and Boston areas, to a Massachusetts company, Premier Executive Transport Services, that until last year was the nominal owner of a Gulfstream executive jet spotted at the scene of post-September 11 'renditions' in Pakistan and Sweden.

Most of the aircraft known to have been used in CIA renditions are executive jets, such as Gulfstreams or Learjets, that are either owned by the agency through front companies like Premier Executive Transport or chartered for upwards of $5,000 an hour.

The plane that carried Abu Omar to Cairo was not a CIA aircraft but a chartered Gulfstream owned by Phillip H. Morse, a multimillionaire Florida businessman and a co-owner of the world champion Boston Red Sox. Morse confirmed to the *Boston Globe* in March that he charters his plane to the CIA and other clients when it is not being used for Red Sox business. But Morse said he knew nothing about the uses to which the intelligence agency had put the plane.

Abu Omar's abduction began on a busy street in broad daylight, as he was walking to a mosque. The startled imam was hustled inside a parked white van that, according to a passer-by, drove away at high speed, followed closely by another vehicle.

The police, who had been keeping tabs on Abu Omar, had no idea where he had gone, although it seemed unlikely that he would have run away from his wife and friends in a country where he had been living lawfully. Abu Omar was granted political asylum by the Italian government after arriving in Milan in 1997, apparently on the grounds that his membership of a radical Egyptian Islamic organisation, *Jamaat al Islamiya*, which he had joined as a university student, left him at risk of political persecution if he returned home to Egypt.

Inspector Bruno Megale, the chief of Milan's police anti-terrorism unit, began the investigation into his disappearance by collecting the numbers of all the cell phones in use in the area where he disappeared. Megale and his investigators looked first for phones that had moved across the Italian cellular network in the direction of Aviano, the site of a large joint US-Italian air base some 175 miles from Milan, where Abu Omar's abductors had put him aboard a Learjet Model LJ-35 that was using the call sign 'SPAR 92.' SPAR is short for Special Air Resources, a military airlift service that uses Learjets and other executive-style jets to transport senior military officers and important civilians.

At 6:20pm on 17 February, SPAR 92, with Abu Omar aboard, departed from Aviano and headed to an air base at Ramstein, Germany, where Abu Omar was moved to the Red Sox Gulfstream. At 8:31pm, the Gulfstream took off and turned southeast, headed for Cairo, where it arrived in the early hours of 18 February.

Records showed that the phones singled out had also been in use at a number of Milan hotels in the weeks preceding the abduction. When the hotel registers were scoured, police learned that a few of the operatives, including the Moldovan-born man, had given the hotels their cell phone numbers. In all, 17 cell phones were identified as belonging to members of the abduction team. Records showed numerous calls among the team members and several others that proved interesting: to a US Air Force colonel at Aviano, to the American Consulate in Milan, and to four numbers in northern Virginia, where the CIA headquarters is.

Fourteen months after Abu Omar disappeared without a trace, the telephone rang in his Milan apartment. His wife, whom Abu Omar married after moving to Italy, still had no clue what had become of her husband. Now she was astounded to hear him explaining that he had just been released from an Egyptian prison, reportedly after a ruling by an Egyptian judge that he was not a terrorist threat.

The police in Milan had continued tapping his telephone in his absence. While their tape recorders turned, Abu Omar told his wife he had been held incommunicado in Egypt since being grabbed off the street in Milan. During that call and in a later conversation with another Egyptian imam in Milan, Mohammed Reda, whose cell phone was also tapped, Abu Omar said he had been tortured by the Egyptian security service.

According to Reda's account of that conversation, published in the Italian newspaper *Corriere della Sera*, Abu Omar 'underwent terrible tortures' after arriving in Cairo. 'He told me that the initial seven months were very tough,' Reda said. 'They hit him day and night. They made him listen to sounds at full blast, which was the reason why his hearing was impaired'.

Shortly after his telephone conversations with his wife and Mohammed Reda, Abu Omar was rearrested by Egyptian authorities. He has not been heard from since'.

Why was Abu Omar abducted?

Why would the US government go to elaborate lengths to seize a 39-year-old Egyptian who, according to former Albanian intelligence officials who have spoken to the *Chicago Tribune*, was once the CIA's most productive source of information within a tightly knit group of Egyptian exiles living in Albania?

One senior US official, who spoke on condition that she not be identified, asserted: 'The world's a better place with this guy off the streets.' But evidence gathered by prosecutors in Italy indicates that the abduction may have been a bold attempt to turn him back into the informer he once was. According to the prosecutor's original application for 13 arrest warrants, made in June 2005, when Abu Omar reached Cairo on a CIA-chartered aircraft, he was taken straight to the Egyptian interior minister. If he agreed to inform for the Egyptian intelligence service, Abu Omar 'would have been set free and accompanied back to Italy,' the document said.

Alternatively, the senior official said, the Americans may have hoped the Egyptians could learn something by interrogating Abu Omar about planned resistance to the impending war on Iraq.

Abu Omar refused to inform, according to the document, and spent the next 14 months in an Egyptian prison facing 'terrible tortures.' After a brief release in April 2004, he was imprisoned again.

The source of the prosecution's information is Mohammed Reda, another Egyptian imam living in Milan and one of the first people Abu Omar called during his brief release. Asked to assess Reda's credibility, the prosecution official asserted that 'in this case, he had no reason to lie. And when he made his first statements, he was unaware he was being intercepted' by a police wiretap on his cell phone.

Abu Omar was first offered a chance to inform in Albania in 1995. According to former officials of ShIK, the Albanian National Intelligence Service, he was far from reluctant. At the behest of the CIA, Albanian Intelligence had created an anti-terrorist unit that, former Albanian officials said, was essentially an arm of the CIA. In those years, the Albanian government, increasingly worried that it might be playing host to Islamic terrorists, accorded the CIA far more leeway than most other countries to operate within its borders.

The real boss of the anti-terror squad, according to its former second-ranking official, Astrit Nasufi, was a CIA officer known as Mike who worked in the American Embassy in Tirana, the Albanian capital. Mike, who spoke fluent Arabic, set up the Albanian Intelligence unit's office and taught Nasufi and the dozen or so other operatives about Islamic terrorism, how to conduct interviews and how to monitor suspects. The CIA even provided the badly paid Albanian agents with better clothes and food for their families, Nasufi said.

Albanian Intelligence sprang into action in August 1995, when the Egyptian foreign minister, Amr Moussa, visited Albania. There was no evidence that an assassination plot against Moussa was in the works. But two months before, exiled Egyptians had tried to kill President Hosni Mubarak during Mubarak's visit to Ethiopia.

Nasufi and Flamur Gjymisha, the chief of the First Intelligence Directorate, said Mike told Albanian Intelligence to detain a dozen or so Egyptians living in Tirana who might pose a threat to Moussa. A few days before Moussa's arrival, Albanian Intelligence got the pick-up list. It included seven or eight members of *Jamaat al Islamiya* ('The Islamic Group') and a few from another Egyptian exile group, the Islamic Jihad, which later was said to have merged with al Qaeda.

Nasufi said Abu Omar, an Egyptian, had been living in Albania for four years and working for a Muslim charity, the Human Relief and Construction Agency (HRCA). His name was not on the pick-up list, Nasufi said, because 'no previous suspicion' had been attached to him, and he had never been mentioned in the CIA's requests for information about individuals in Tirana.

The CIA also gave Albanian Intelligence the licence plate numbers of four cars, including a dark green Land Rover that allegedly belonged to the Human Relief and Construction Agency. 'We started looking for the cars on August 27 in the morning,' recalled Nasufi. By mid-afternoon they had found the Land Rover in a parking lot near the former Institute for Physical Education. When Albanian Intelligence checked the registration, the person listed as responsible for the vehicle was Osama Nasr – Abu Omar.

According to Nasufi, the Land Rover looked like it hadn't been driven for months. Nevertheless, two CIA operatives arrived from the United States and checked the vehicle for any trace of explosives. Nothing was found, Nasufi said, but the CIA told Albanian Intelligence to pick up Abu Omar anyway. Around 10 pm on August 27, Albanian police showed up at Abu Omar's Tirana apartment and led him away. He was held for about 10 days, Nasufi said.

What was essentially an accidental arrest proved to be a great coup for Albanian Intelligence and its CIA overseers. Abu Omar was taken to the main police station for interrogation by Nasufi and another Albanian Intelligence agent, Ferdinand Nuku. Nasufi described Abu Omar as 'smooth and calm, probably because he wasn't under pressure from us. He was never aggressive with us. We didn't use a lot of physical pressure on him. He was well-behaved and gentle.'

At first Abu Omar refused to talk, then abruptly changed his mind. 'After a week, we had a full file,' said Nasufi, who doesn't remember Abu Omar as a particularly zealous Muslim, recalling that he interrupted the interviews to pray only twice in 10 days.

To Albanian Intelligence, Abu Omar admitted he had fled Egypt because he belonged to *Jamaat al Islamiya*, and that *Jamaat* had about 10 people working for three Islamic charities in Albania, including the Al-Haramain Islamic Foundation and the Revival of Islamic Heritage Society.

Abu Omar told the Albanian Intelligence agents that, for *Jamaat* members like himself, Albania was a 'safe hotel' – a country where fundamentalist Muslims believed they could live without fear of political repression. For that reason, Abu Omar insisted, the *Jamaat* members in Albania had no plans to kill Amr Moussa. Such a move would have cost *Jamaat* its haven, Abu Omar explained.

Abu Omar was the first Arab willing to inform to Albanian Intelligence, which was amazed by its good fortune. So, Nasufi said, was the CIA. After each interview, Nuku gave handwritten notes to the US Embassy's new CIA representative, 'Francis,' who had replaced 'Mike.' 'It was the first case that we provided the Americans with totally independent information,' Nasufi said. 'We became a main player for the first time. We weren't just tools. We gave them a clear idea of who was monitoring the US Embassy for [*Jamaat*], who was coming in and out of the country.'

At the time, the CIA in the Balkans was primarily interested in keeping tabs on the former *mujahedeen* joining the Bosnian Muslims in their struggle against Serbia and Croatia.

Nasufi said Abu Omar was believed to be credible. Of the 100 or so items of information he offered, 20 or 30 were confirmed by information Albanian Intelligence received from the CIA. After Abu Omar was allowed to return home, the collaboration deepened. He talked to ShIK about *Jamaat* branches in the United Kingdom, Germany and Italy – including Milan, where *Jamaat* had close relations with the Institute for Islamic Studies on Via Quaranta.

ShIK had a strict rule against offering money to informers, Nasufi said, but ShIK did offer Abu Omar help in mediating a dispute with the landlord of the bakery he had just opened, and smoothing out problems with his residence permit that had arisen from his marriage to an Albanian, Marsela Glina. Abu Omar gratefully accepted ShIK's help, Nasufi said. But a few weeks after he began collaborating with ShIK, Abu Omar, Marsela and their daughter Sara suddenly left Albania. Abu Omar's hasty departure struck ShIK as odd, Nasufi recalled, because the Egyptian had seemed so willing to cooperate and had appeared happy that ShIK was offering him assistance with his problems. When Flamur Gjymisha asked Ferdinand Nuku what had happened to Abu Omar, Nuku said the CIA had told him Abu Omar was living in Germany.

Abu Omar, without his Albanian family, surfaced again in Rome in 1997, where he was accorded political refugee status. Moving north to Milan, he gravitated to the Islamic Institute on Via Quaranta. There Abu Omar served for a time as the deputy chief imam.

According to what the police were hearing on his telephone, Abu Omar also was helping recruit Muslims to fight against the coalition in Afghanistan. A Milan magistrate recently ruled in an unrelated case that recruiting fighters for foreign battles is not illegal under Italy's anti-terrorist laws. Nor, it seems, did the police have much evidence that Abu Omar had been plotting terrorist attacks.

When Milan prosecutors applied for an arrest warrant for Abu Omar, the only charges listed were 'association with terrorists,' aiding the preparation of false documents and abetting illegal immigration. Although police had grounds for Abu Omar's arrest, the tap on his phone and the microphones hidden in his apartment and the Via Quaranta mosque made him far more valuable as a window into the comings and goings of other jihadists. 'When you find an important member of an organisation,' the senior prosecution official said, 'you don't arrest him immediately, you follow him. When Nasr disappeared in February [2003], our investigation came to a standstill.'

What mystified the Italian authorities was why the CIA would want to take Abu Omar out of circulation – especially since they were sharing with the CIA the fruits of their electronic surveillance of Abu Omar – and why the Egyptians would want him back.

Extraordinary Rendition
Case Study III

Khaled El-Masri's story

Khaled El-Masri, a German citizen, was detained in Macedonia whilst going on holiday, and rendered to Afghanistan by the Americans where he was held for months at the 'Salt Pit'.

These excerpts are taken from Mr El-Masri's complaint against George J Tenet [former head of the CIA], Premier Executive Transport Services, Inc and other defendants brought in the United States District Court for the Eastern District of Virginia, dated 6 December 2005.

Plaintiff Khaled El-Masri was born in Kuwait in 1963, and raised in Lebanon. He fled Lebanon in 1985 to escape the civil war in that country, and settled in Germany, where he became a citizen in 1995. He attended high school for three years before leaving to become a carpenter. He has since been employed as a truck driver and a car salesman, but has been unemployed since the conclusion of the events described below. Mr. El-Masri is married and has five young children.

On December 31, 2003, Mr. El-Masri boarded a bus in Ulm, Germany, intending to visit Skopje, Macedonia, for a brief holiday. Mr. El-Masri's journey was uneventful, passing through several European border inspections without incident, until the bus crossed the Serbian border into Macedonia. There, Macedonian law enforcement officials confiscated Mr. El-Masri's passport and detained him for several hours. He was thereafter transferred by armed plainclothes officers to a hotel in Skopje.

Mr. El-Masri was detained in the hotel for 23 days, guarded at all hours by rotating shifts of armed Macedonian officers. The curtains were closed day and night, and Mr. El-Masri was never permitted to leave the room. His frequent requests to see a lawyer, translator, or German consular official, or to contact his wife, were denied. When he once moved toward the door and stated that he intended to leave, three of his captors pointed pistols at his head and threatened to shoot him.

Mr. El-Masri was interrogated repeatedly by Macedonian agents throughout the course of his detention. The interrogations were conducted in English, despite Mr. El-Masri's limited English proficiency. He was questioned about what he did in Ulm, the persons with whom he associated there, and the persons who attended his mosque, the Ulm Multicultural Centre and Mosque. Mr. El-Masri's interrogators pressed him continuously about a meeting he allegedly had in Jalalabad, Afghanistan with an Egyptian man, and about possible Norwegian contacts. Mr. El-Masri responded that he had never been to Jalalabad and knew no one from Norway.

On the seventh day of his confinement, a man who appeared to be in charge of the interrogators proposed to Mr. El-Masri that if he confessed his involvement with al Qaeda, he would be returned to Germany. Mr. El-Masri refused. On the thirteenth day of his confinement, Mr. El-Masri commenced a hunger strike to protest his continued unlawful detention, and he did not eat again during the remaining ten days of detention in Macedonia.

On January 23, 2004, seven or eight Macedonian men dressed in civilian clothes whom Mr. El-Masri had not seen before entered the hotel room. The men recorded a 15-minute video of Mr. El-Masri. They instructed him to say that he had been treated well, had not been harmed in any way, and would shortly be flown back to Germany. The men then handcuffed and blindfolded him and placed him in a car.

After a drive of approximately one hour, the car came to a halt, and Mr. El-Masri could hear the sound of airplanes. He was removed from the vehicle, still handcuffed and blindfolded, and was led to a building. Inside, he was told that he would be medically examined. Instead, he was beaten severely from all sides with fists and what felt like a thick stick. His clothes were sliced from his body with scissors or a knife, leaving him in his underwear. He was told to remove his underwear and he refused. He was beaten again, and his underwear was forcibly removed. He heard the sound of pictures being taken. He was thrown to the floor. His hands were pulled back and a boot was placed on his back. He then felt a firm object being forced into his anus.

Mr. El-Masri was pulled from the floor and dragged to a corner of the room. His blindfold was removed. A flash went off and temporarily blinded him. When he recovered his sight, he saw seven or eight men dressed in black and wearing black ski masks. One of the men placed him in a diaper. He was then dressed in a dark blue short-sleeved track suit, and placed in a belt with chains that attached to his wrists and ankles. The men put earmuffs and eye pads on him, blindfolded him, and hooded him.

Mr. El-Masri was marched to a waiting plane, with the shackles cutting into his ankles. Once inside, he was thrown to the floor face down and his legs and arms were spread-eagled and secured to the sides of the plane. He felt an injection in his shoulder, and became lightheaded. He felt a second injection that rendered him nearly unconscious.

On information and belief, the men dressed in black clothing and ski masks were members of a CIA 'black renditions' team, operating pursuant to unlawful CIA policies and at the direction of defendant Tenet.

Mr. El-Masri was dimly aware of the plane landing and taking off again. When the plane landed for the final time, he was unchained and taken off the plane. It was warmer outside than it had been in Macedonia, and Mr. El-Masri realized that he had not been returned to Germany. He believed he might be in Guantánamo, or possibly Iraq. He learned later that he was in Afghanistan.

Aviation documents show that a Boeing business jet owned by defendant Premier Executive Transport Services and operated by defendant Aero Contractors Ltd, then registered by the Federal Aviation Authority as N313P, took off from Palma, Majorca, Spain on January 23, 2004, and landed at the Skopje airport at 8:51 p.m. that evening. The jet left Skopje more than three hours later, flying to Baghdad and then on to Kabul, the Afghan capital. On Sunday, January 25, the jet left Kabul, flying to Timisoara, Romania.

Mr. El-Masri was removed from the plane and shoved into the back of a waiting vehicle. The car drove for about ten minutes. Mr. El-Masri was then dragged from the vehicle, pushed into a building, thrown to the floor, and kicked and beaten on the head and the small of his back. He was left in a small, dirty, concrete cell. When he adjusted his eyes to the light, he saw that the walls were covered in crude Arabic, Urdu, and Farsi writing. The cell did not contain a bed. It was cold, but Mr. El-Masri had been provided only one dirty, military-style blanket and some old, torn clothes bundled into a thin pillow. Through a window at the top of the cell, Mr. El-Masri saw a red, setting sun, and realised that he had been travelling for 24 hours.

On information and belief, the prison to which Mr. El-Masri was transferred was a CIA-run facility known as the 'Salt Pit,' an abandoned brick factory north of the Kabul business district that was used by the CIA for detention of some high-level terror suspects.

Mr. El-Masri was thirsty. Through the small, barred window of his cell, Mr. El-Masri saw a man dressed in Afghan clothing. He shouted to the man for water, and the man pointed to a bottle of putrid water in the corner of the cell. Mr. El-Masri asked for fresh water, but was told he could drink from the bottle or go thirsty.

That night, Mr. El-Masri was removed from his cell and transferred to an interrogation room. There were six or eight men dressed in the same black clothing and ski masks as the men in the Macedonian airport, as well as a masked doctor who spoke American-accented English and a translator who spoke Arabic with a Palestinian accent. Mr. El-Masri was stripped naked, photographed, and medically examined by one of the masked men. Blood and urine samples were taken. Mr. El-Masri complained to the man who seemed to be a doctor about the unhygienic water and poor conditions in his cell. The man responded that the Afghans were responsible for the conditions of his confinement. Then Mr. El-Masri was returned to his cell, where he would be detained in a single-person cell, with no reading or writing materials, and without once being permitted outside to breathe fresh air, for more than four months.

On his second night in the Salt Pit, Mr. El-Masri was woken by masked men and once again brought to the interrogation room. Again, six or eight masked, black-clad men were in the room. Mr. El-Masri was interrogated by a masked man who spoke Arabic with a South Lebanese accent. The man asked him if he knew why he had been detained; Mr. El-Masri said he did not. The man then stated that Mr. El-Masri was in a country with no laws, and that no one knew where he was, and asked whether Mr. El-Masri understood what that meant.

Mr. El-Masri was interrogated about whether he had taken a trip to Jalalabad using a false passport; whether he had attended Palestinian training camps; whether he was acquainted with September 11 conspirators Mohammed Atta and Ramzi Binalshibh; and whether he associated with alleged extremists in Ulm, Germany. Mr. El-Masri, who has never knowingly associated with any terrorist or terrorist organisation, answered these questions truthfully, just as he had in Macedonia. Mr. El-Masri asked why he had been transported to Afghanistan, when he was a German citizen with no ties to that country. His interrogator did not answer.

In all, Mr. El-Masri was interrogated on three or four occasions, each time by the same man, and each time at night. His interrogations were accompanied by threats, insults, pushing, and shoving. Two men who participated in the interrogations identified themselves as Americans. Mr. El-Masri repeatedly demanded that he be permitted to meet with a representative of the German government, but these requests were ignored.

In March, Mr. El-Masri and several other inmates with whom he communicated through cell walls commenced a hunger strike to protest their continued confinement without charges. After 27 days without food, Mr. El-Masri was given an audience with two unmasked Americans, one of whom was the prison director and the second an even higher official whom other inmates referred to as 'the Boss.' The Afghan prison director was also present, along with the translator with the Palestinian accent. Mr. El-Masri insisted that the Americans either release him, bring him before a court, allow him access to a German official, or watch him starve to death. The American prison director replied that he could not release Mr. El-Masri without permission from Washington, but stated that Mr. El-Masri should not be detained in the prison. Mr. El-Masri was returned to his cell, where he continued his hunger strike.

Mr. El-Masri's health deteriorated on a daily basis. He received no medical treatment during his confinement, despite repeated requests.

On information and belief, CIA officials at the 'Salt Pit' believed early on that they had detained the wrong person. In March, Mr. El-Masri's passport was examined by CIA officials in Langley, Virginia and determined to be valid. Defendant Tenet was notified in April that the CIA had detained the wrong person. By early May, Condoleezza Rice, then the President's National Security Advisor, had been informed that the CIA was detaining an innocent German citizen. Nonetheless, Mr. El-Masri was detained in the 'Salt Pit' until May 28.

On the thirty-seventh day of his hunger strike, hooded men entered Mr. El-Masri's cell, dragged him from his bed, and bound his hands and feet. They dragged him into the interrogation room, sat him on a chair, and tied him to it. A feeding tube was then forced through his nose to his stomach and a liquid was poured through it. After this procedure, Mr. El-Masri was given some canned food as well as some books to read. Mr. El-Masri was weighed. Since the time of his seizure in December of 2003, Mr. El-Masri had lost more than sixty pounds.

Following his force-feeding, Mr. El-Masri became extremely ill and suffered very severe pain. A doctor visited Mr. El-Masri's cell in the middle of the night and administered medication, but Mr. El-Masri remained bedridden for several days.

Around the beginning of May, the prison director brought Mr. El-Masri to the interrogation room, where he met an American who identified himself as a psychologist, accompanied by a female interpreter with a Syrian accent. The psychologist told Mr. El-Masri that he had travelled from Washington DC to check on him and ask him some questions. At the conclusion of the conversation, the man promised that Mr. El-Masri would be released from the facility very soon.

Soon thereafter, Mr. El-Masri was visited by a German speaker who identified himself only as 'Sam.' 'Sam' was accompanied by the American prison director and an American translator. Mr. El-Masri asked 'Sam' whether he was a representative of the German government, and whether the German government knew that Mr. El-Masri was being held in Afghanistan, but 'Sam,' after consulting with the Americans, declined to answer. He asked 'Sam' whether his wife knew where he was; 'Sam' replied that she did not. 'Sam' then proceeded to ask Mr. El-Masri many of the same questions he had previously been asked regarding his alleged associations with extremists in Neu Ulm, Germany.

'Sam' visited Mr. El-Masri three more times. In late May, Mr. El-Masri received a visit from 'Sam,' the American prison director, and an American doctor. He was informed that he would be released in eight days. 'Sam' warned him that, as a condition of his release, he was never to mention what had happened to him, because the Americans were determined to keep the affair a secret.

On May 27, the American doctor visited Mr. El-Masri's cell. He instructed Mr. El-Masri not to eat or drink anything, as the next day he would be transported back to Germany, and during the transit back, he would not be permitted to use the bathroom. The next morning, the doctor and the American prison director arrived in his cell. Mr. El-Masri was blindfolded and cuffed, led out of his cell, and driven for about ten minutes. He was then locked in what seemed to be a shipping container until he heard the sound of an aircraft arriving.

Mr. El-Masri was released from the shipping container, and his belongings were returned to him. He was told to change back into the clothes he had worn in Macedonia, and was given two new t-shirts. He was then driven to the waiting plane, blindfolded and ear-muffed, and led onto the plane, where he was chained to his seat.

The man named 'Sam' accompanied Mr. El-Masri on the plane. Mr. El-Masri also heard the muffled voices of two or three Americans. Shortly after take-off, Mr. El-Masri asked 'Sam' if he could have the earmuffs removed; 'Sam' obliged, after consulting with the Americans. Sam informed Mr. El-Masri that Germany had a new President. He said that the plane would land in a European country other than Germany, because the Americans did not want to leave clear traces of their involvement in Mr. El-Masri's ordeal, but that Mr. El-Masri would eventually continue on to Germany. Mr. El-Masri feared that he would not be returned home, but rather taken to another country and executed.

When the plane landed, Mr. El-Masri, still blindfolded, was taken off the plane and placed in the back seat of a vehicle. He was not told where he was. He was driven in the vehicle up and down mountains, on paved and unpaved roads, for more than three hours. The vehicle came to a halt, and Mr. El-Masri was aware of the men in the car getting out and closing the doors, and then of men climbing into the vehicle. All of the men had Slavic-sounding accents but said very little.

The vehicle proceeded to drive for another three hours, again up and down mountains and on paved and unpaved roads. Eventually, the vehicle was brought to a halt. Mr. El-Masri was taken from the car, and his blindfold was removed. His captors gave him his belongings and passport, removed his handcuffs, and directed him to walk down the path without turning back. It was dark, and the road was deserted. Mr. El-Masri believed he would be shot in the back and left to die.

Mr. El-Masri rounded a corner and came across three armed men. They immediately asked for his passport. They saw that his German passport had no visa in it, and asked him why he was in Albania without legal permission. Mr. El-Masri replied that he had no idea where he was. He was told that he was near the borders with Macedonia and Serbia. The men led Mr. El-Masri to a small building with an Albanian flag, and he was presented to a superior officer. The officer observed Mr. El-Masri's long hair and long beard and told him he looked like a terrorist. Mr. El-Masri asked to be taken to the German embassy, but the man told him he would be taken to the airport instead.

Mr. El-Masri was driven to the Mother Theresa Airport in Tirana, arriving at about 6am. One of the Albanian guards took his passport and 320 Euros from his wallet and went into the airport building. When he returned, he instructed Mr. El-Masri to go through a door, where he was met by a person who guided him through customs and immigration control without inspection. Only after the plane was airborne did Mr. El-Masri finally believe he was returning to Germany.

The plane landed at Frankfurt International Airport at 8:40am. Mr. El-Masri was by then about forty pounds lighter than when he had left Germany, his hair was long and unkempt, and he had not shaved since his arrival in Macedonia. From Frankfurt he travelled to Ulm, and from there to his home outside the city. His house was empty and clearly had been so for some time. He proceeded to the Cultural Center in Neu Ulm and asked after his wife and children. He was told that his family had relocated to Lebanon when he failed to return from his holiday.

In June 2004, having been notified by Mr. El-Masri's German lawyer, the Office of the Prosecuting Magistrate in Munich, Germany opened an investigation into Mr. El-Masri's allegations that he had been unlawfully abducted, detained, and interrogated in Macedonia and Afghanistan. German officials easily corroborated Mr. El-Masri's account that he had travelled to Macedonia and had been detained shortly after entering that country. To evaluate Mr. El-Masri's account of his detention in Afghanistan, German authorities conducted scientific tests, including radioactive isotope analysis of Mr. El-Masri's hair. Those tests were consistent with Mr. El-Masri's account that he had spent time in a South Asian country and had been deprived of food for an extended period.

Extraordinary Rendition Case Study IV

Omar Deghayes' story

Jackie Chase

Jackie Chase of the Save Omar Deghayes Campaign briefed the European Network on Peace and Human Rights at its meeting at the European Parliament in Brussels in October 2005 about Omar's continuing detention in Guantánamo Bay. Here she tells his story of abduction from Pakistan, and recounts the cases of some other British residents held at Guantánamo Bay.

Omar Deghayes is 35 years old. He is a Libyan citizen who has had refugee status in the United Kingdom since 1987. He has been detained in Guantánamo Bay for more than three years. He was arrested in Pakistan in April 2002, apparently for a bounty of $5,000, and transferred to Guantánamo Bay five months later.

Since arriving in Guantánamo, Mr Deghayes has been blinded in one eye. There are credible reports that he has been tortured. He has not been charged with any crime. He is one of nine British residents still held in Guantánamo.

The Save Omar Deghayes Campaign calls for the immediate return to the United Kingdom of all nine British non-nationals detained in Guantánamo Bay. They are Omar Deghayes, Bisher al-Rawi, Jamal el Banna, Benyam Mohammed, Shaker Aamer, Jamal Kiyemba, Ahmed Errachiddi, Ahmed Ben Bacha and Abdelnour Sameur.

In 1997, Britain recognised Jamal el Banna as a refugee from Jordan. His wife and five children are all British citizens. Bisher al-Rawi's family has lived in the United Kingdom for 20 years. They are all British citizens excepting Bisher himself, who has long been recognised as a refugee. His family fled Iraq after Bisher's father had been detained and tortured by Saddam Hussein's regime. The allegations that Britain is co-operating with the 'rendition' system are bolstered by the story behind Bisher and Jamal's arrests in Gambia. The two men were seized at Banjul airport after a tip-off from the British, having travelled there on business to do with a mobile peanut processing plant. They were immediately handed over to US authorities. Bisher and Jamal had already been interviewed in London by MI5, Britain's domestic security service, but they had not been detained. In Gambia, when Bisher al Rawi asked to see the British High Commissioner, he said he was told: 'Who do you think ordered your arrest?'

The situation of these men is made all the more urgent in light of recent reports of the escalation of the hunger strike at Guantánamo Bay. The United Nations reports that the hunger-strikers may have been forced fed.

Abubaker Deghayes, brother of Omar Deghayes, said:

> '30 years ago Amnesty International issued an urgent action in relation to my father, and now has had to do the same thing for Omar. We were granted asylum in Britain when my father was assassinated by the Libyan police. Omar needs a place of safety now more than ever. I am now a British citizen, as my brother would be, if he had not been illegally detained by the United States. Our home is Brighton, whose people have so kindly supported the campaign for Omar's release.'

Mrs S. El-Banna, wife of Guantánamo detainee Jamal El Banna, said:

> 'My third son got a prize at school for being a super citizen. The first person he thought of was his dad. He said, how can I tell him I'm a super citizen?'

TRANSPORT & GENERAL WORKERS' UNION
London, South East & East Anglia

Let's make 2006 a year of success for a

TRADE UNION FREEDOM BILL

For trade union rights in the UK and around the world

Eddie McDermott
Regional Secretary

John Childs
Regional Chair

(phone)
020. 8800. 4281

(email)
emcdermott@tgwu.org.uk

(fax)
020. 8802. 8388

**Extraordinary Rendition
The new interrogators
Case Study V**

Soldiers out of Control

Human Rights Watch

Human Rights Watch recorded these accounts given by US personnel of the 82nd Airborne Division, from which we reprint excerpts. They concern the treatment of 'Persons Under Control' (PUCs) – prisoners who were entrusted to the care of the military. The full report, published in September 2005, is available online (www.hrw.org).

Sergeant A's Account

Sergeant A served in Afghanistan from September 2002 to March 2003 and in Iraq from August 2003 to April 2004. Human Rights Watch spoke with him on four separate occasions in July and August 2005.

In retrospect what we did was wrong, but at the time we did what we had to do. Everything we did was accepted, everyone turned their heads.

We got to the camp in August [2003] and set up. We started to go out on missions right away. We didn't start taking persons under control (PUCs) until September. Shit started to go bad right away. On my very first guard shift for my first interrogation that I observed was the first time I saw a person under control pushed to the brink of a stroke or heart attack. At first I was surprised, like, this is what we are allowed to do? This is what we are allowed to get away with? I think the officers knew about it but didn't want to hear about it. They didn't want to know it even existed. But they had to.

On a normal day I was on shift in a person under control tent. When we got these guys we had them sandbagged and zip tied, meaning we had a sandbag on their heads and zip ties [plastic cuffs] on their hands. We took their belongings and tossed them in the person under control tent. We were told why they were there. If I was told they were there sitting on IEDs [Improvised Explosive Devices, homemade bombs] we would fuck them up, put them in stress positions or put them in a tent and withhold water.

The 'Murderous Maniacs' was what they called us at our camp because they knew if they got caught by us and got detained by us before they went to Abu Ghraib then it would be hell to pay. They would be just, you know, you couldn't even imagine. It was sort of like I told you when they came in it was like a game. You know, how far could you make this guy go before he passes out or just collapses on you. From stress positions to keeping them up fucking two days straight, whatever. Deprive them of food, water, whatever.

To 'Fuck a PUC' means to beat him up. We would give them blows to the head, chest, legs, and stomach, pull them down, kick dirt on them. This happened every day.

To 'smoke' someone is to put them in stress positions until they get muscle fatigue and pass out. That happened every day. Some days we would just get bored so we would have everyone sit in a corner and then make them get in a pyramid. This was before Abu Ghraib, but just like it. We did that for amusement.

Guard shifts were four hours. We would stress them at least in excess of twelve hours. When I go off shift and the next guy comes we are already stressing the person under control and we let the new guy know what he did and to keep fucking him. We put five-gallon water cans and made them hold them out to where they got muscle fatigue, then made them do push-ups and jumping jacks until they passed out. We would withhold water for whole guard shifts. And the next guy would, too. Then you gotta take them to the john if you give them water and that was a pain. And we withheld food, giving them the bare minimum like crackers from MREs [Meals Ready to Eat, the military's pre-packaged food]. And sleep deprivation was a really big thing.

Someone from [Military Intelligence] told us these guys don't get no sleep. They were directed to get intel [intelligence] from them, so we had to set the conditions by banging on their cages, crashing them into the cages, kicking them, kicking dirt, yelling. All that shit. We never stripped them down because this is an all-guy base and that is fucked up shit. We poured cold water on them all the time to where they were soaking wet and we would cover them in dirt and sand. We did the jugs of water where they held them out to collapse all the time. The water and other shit... start[ed] [m]aybe late September, early October 2003. This was all at Camp Mercury ... like 10 minutes from Fallujah. We would transport the persons under control from Mercury to Abu Ghraib.

None of this happened in Afghanistan. We had MPs [military police] attached to us in Afghanistan so we didn't deal with prisoners. We had no MPs in Iraq. We had to secure prisoners. [Military intelligence] wants to interrogate them and they had to provide guards, so we would be the guards. I did missions every day and always came back with 10-15 prisoners. We were told by intel that these guys were bad, but they could be wrong, sometimes they were wrong. I would be told, 'These guys were improvised explosive devices trigger men last week.' So we would fuck them up. Fuck them up bad. If I was told the guy was caught with a 9mm [handgun] in his car, we wouldn't fuck them up too bad – just a little. If we were on patrol and catch a guy that killed my captain or my buddy last week – man, it is human nature. So we fucked them up bad. At the same time we should be held to a higher standard. I know that now. It was wrong. There are a set of standards. But you gotta understand, this was the norm. Everyone would just sweep it under the rug.

What you allowed to happen happened. Trends were accepted. Leadership failed to provide clear guidance so we just developed it. They wanted intel. As long as no persons under control came up dead it happened. We heard rumours of persons under control dying so we were careful. We kept it to broken arms and legs and shit. If a leg was broken you call the PA – the physician's assistant – and told him the person under control got hurt when he was taken. He would get Motrin [a pain reliever] and maybe a sling, but no cast or medical treatment.

In Afghanistan we were attached to Special Forces and saw OGA ('Other Governmental Agency' – a term that is frequently used to refer to the CIA). We never interacted with them but they would stress guys. We learned how to do it. We saw it when we would guard an interrogation.

I was an Infantry Fire Team Leader. The majority of the time I was out on mission. When not on mission I was riding the persons under control. We should have had military police. We should have taken them to Abu Ghraib [which] was only 15 fucking minutes drive. But there was no one to talk to in the chain – it just got killed. We would talk among ourselves, say, 'This is bad.' But no one listened. We should never have been allowed to watch guys we had fought.

Forward Operating Base Mercury was about as big as a football field. We had a battalion there with three or four companies and attachments. We lived in the buildings of an old Iraqi military compound that we built up with barriers, ACs [air conditioners], and stuff. We had civilian interpreters on post and contractors came every day to fix shit. The contractors were local Iraqis.

The persons under control lived in the person under control area about 200 metres away. It had a triple-strength circle concertina barrier with tents in the middle with another triple-strength concertina perimeter. Inside each was a Hesco basket that is wire that normally has cloth in it. We filled them with dirt to make barriers and some we emptied and buried to use as access points for the Iraqis. This was all inside the confines of the Forward Operating Base. There was a guard tower behind the person under control tent with two guards. One was always looking at the person under control tent. We never took direct fire, but did take regular rocket and mortar attacks. We did not lose anyone, but had shrapnel injuries.

On their day off people would show up all the time. Everyone in camp knew if you wanted to work out your frustration you show up at the person under control tent. In a way it was sport. The cooks were all US soldiers. One day a sergeant shows up and tells a person under control to grab a pole. He told him to bend over and broke the guy's leg with a mini Louisville Slugger that was a metal bat. He was the fucking cook. He shouldn't be in with no persons under control. The physician's assistant came and said to keep him off the leg. Three days later they transported the person under control to Abu Ghraib. The Louisville Slugger [incident] happened around November 2003, certainly before Christmas.

People would just volunteer just to get their frustrations out. We had guys from all over the base just come to guard persons under control so they could fuck them up. Broken bones didn't happen too often, maybe every other week. The physician's assistant would overlook it. I am sure they knew.

The interrogator [a sergeant] worked in the [intelligence] office. He was former

Special Forces. He would come into the person under control tent and request a guy by number. Everyone was tagged. He would say, 'Give me no. 22.' And we would bring him out. He would smoke the guy and fuck him. He would always say to us, 'You didn't see anything, right?' And we would always say, 'No, Sergeant.'

One day a soldier came to the person under control tent to get his aggravation out and filled his hands with dirt and hit a person under control in the face. He fucked him. That was the communications guy.

One night a guy came and broke chem lights open and beat the persons under control with it. That made them glow in the dark, which was real funny, but it burned their eyes and their skin was irritated real bad.

If a person under control cooperated Intel would tell us that he was allowed to sleep or got extra food. If he felt the person under control was lying he told us he doesn't get any fucking sleep and gets no food except maybe crackers. And he tells us to smoke him. [Intel] would tell the Lieutenant that he had to smoke the prisoners and that is what we were told to do. No sleep, water, and just crackers. That's it. The point of doing all this was to get them ready for interrogation. [The intelligence officer] said he wanted the persons under control so fatigued, so smoked, so demoralised that they want to cooperate. But half of these guys got released because they didn't do nothing. We sent them back to Fallujah. But if he's a good guy, you know, now he's a bad guy because of the way we treated him.

After Abu Ghraib things toned down. We still did it but we were careful. It is still going on now the same way, I am sure. Maybe not as blatant but it is how we do things.

Each company goes out on a mission and you kick the door down and catch them red handed. We caught them with rocket propelled grenades. So we are going to give you special attention. We yank them off the truck and they hit the ground hard, maybe 5-6 feet down. We took everything and searched them. Then we toss him in the person under control tent with a sandbag on his head and he is zip tied. And he is like that all day and it is 100 degrees in that tent. Once paperwork was done we started to stress them …

We had these new high-speed trailer showers. One guy was the cleaner. He was an Iraqi contractor working on base. We were taking pretty accurate mortar fire and rockets and we were getting nervous. Well one day we found him with a global positioning satellite receiver and he is like calling in strikes on us! What the fuck!? We took him but we are pissed because he stabbed us in the back. So we gave him the treatment. We got on him with the jugs and doused him and smoked and fucked him.

Officer C's Account

C is an officer with the 82nd Airborne Division and West Point graduate who served in Afghanistan from August 2002 to February 2003 and in Iraq from September 2003 to March 2004. Human Rights Watch spoke with him more than two dozen times in July, August, and September 2005. Below are excerpts from those interviews grouped by subject matter (the subject headings were supplied by Human Rights Watch).

On conditions at Forward Operating Base Mercury

When we were at Forward Operating Base Mercury, we had prisoners that were stacked in pyramids, not naked but they were stacked in pyramids. We had prisoners that were forced to do extremely stressful exercises for at least two hours at a time which personally I am in good shape and I would not be able to do that type of exercises for two hours ... There was a case where a prisoner had cold water dumped on him and then he was left outside in the night. Again, exposure to elements. There was a case where a soldier took a baseball bat and struck a detainee on the leg hard. This is all stuff that I'm getting from my non-commissioned officers.

In the person under control holding facility you could have had people that could have been in the wrong house at the wrong time brought in and all of a sudden they are subjected to this. So that's a big problem, obviously a huge human rights issue.

It's army doctrine that when you take a prisoner, one of the things you do is secure that prisoner and then you speed him to the rear. You get him out of the hands of the unit that took him. Well, we didn't do that. We'd keep them out at holding facility for I think it was up to seventy-two hours. Then we would place him under the guard of soldiers he had just been trying to kill. The incident with the detainee hit with a baseball bat; he was suspected of having killed one of our officers.

[At FOB Mercury] they said that they had pictures that were similar to what happened at Abu Ghraib, and because they were so similar to what happened at Abu Ghraib, the soldiers destroyed the pictures. They burned them. The exact quote was, 'They [the soldiers at Abu Ghraib] were getting in trouble for the same things we were told to do, so we destroyed the pictures.'

Frustration with the military chain of command

I witnessed violations of the Geneva Conventions that I knew were violations of the Geneva Conventions when they happened, but I was under the impression that that was US policy at the time. And as soon as Abu Ghraib broke, and they had hearings in front of Congress, the Secretary of Defence testified that we followed the spirit of the Geneva Conventions in Afghanistan, and the letter of the Geneva Conventions in Iraq, and as soon as he said that I knew something was wrong. So I called some of my classmates [from West Point], confirmed what I was concerned about, and then on that Monday morning I approached my chain of command.

I talked to an officer in the Ranger regiment and his response was, he wouldn't tell me exactly what he witnessed but he said 'I witnessed things that were more intense than what you witnessed,' but it wasn't anything that exceeded what I had heard about at Survival, Evasion, Resistance, Escape School. After that I called the chaplain at West Point who I respected a lot and I talked to him about some things and we were on the same page. Then I had said well, 'I'm going to talk to my company commander and then my battalion commander on Monday.'

My company commander said, 'I see how you can take it that way, but…' he said something like, 'remember the honour of the unit is at stake' or something to that effect and 'Don't expect me to go to bat for you on this issue if you take this up,' something to that effect.

I went and talked to my battalion commander. Again, he clearly thinks he has done the right things and that what I am bringing attention to is within the standards and that he is okay. He didn't dismiss me. He just said 'Go talk to Judge Advocate General (JAG). We'll work this out.' It wasn't alarming to him in any way, shape or form that these things had happened.

So I went to the Judge Advocate General and … he says, 'Well the Geneva Conventions are a grey area.' So I mentioned some things that I had heard about and said, 'Is it a violation to chain prisoners to the ground naked for the purpose of interrogations?' and he said, 'That's within the Geneva Conventions.' So I said, 'Okay. That is within the Geneva Conventions.' And then there is the prisoner on the box with the wires attached to him, and to me, as long as electricity didn't go through the wires, that was in accordance with what I would have expected US policy to be, and that he wasn't under the threat of death. And he said, 'Well, that is a clear violation of the Geneva Conventions.' And I said, 'Okay, but I'm looking for some kind of standard here to be able to tell what I should stop and what I should allow to happen.' And he says, 'Well, we've had questions about that at times.'

Then he said, 'There was a device that another battalion in the 82nd had come up with that you would put a prisoner in. It was uncomfortable to sit in.' And he went to test it out by sitting in it and he decided that it wasn't torture. I hear this and I am flabbergasted that this is the standard the Army is using to determine whether or not we follow the Geneva Conventions. If I go to the Judge Advocate General and he cannot give me clear guidance about what I should stop and what I should allow to happen, how is a non-commissioned officer or a private expected to act appropriately?

When I talked to [an official in the Inspector General's office about the policy confusion on what was permitted] he says, 'You obviously feel very upset about this, but – I don't think you're going to accomplish anything because things don't stick to people inside the Beltway [Washington, D.C.].' He says, 'I worked at the Pentagon and things don't stick to people inside the Beltway.'

When the Secretary of the Army came [to my training], I addressed him on numerous issues, which I don't want to go into. One of those issues was treatment of prisoners. I mentioned that I didn't have clear guidance, and the Secretary of the Army said, 'Well, we realised that that was a problem but you are a little bit behind the times. We've solved that matter. And I didn't get a chance to respond to that. I should have, I should have pressed that issue a lot harder. That's one of my regrets. Just bringing up the issue at all was stressful, but it hasn't been resolved because there is no clear guidance. And through discussions with other officers the problem is not taken care of. It really is multiple problems. It's two problems. One is the Army handling interrogations, and the other is the relationship between Other Governmental Agency (CIA) and prisoners and what they can and can't do.

Confusion within the ranks on coercive interrogation

[In Afghanistan,] I thought that the chain of command all the way up to the National Command Authority [The President of the United States and the Secretary of Defence] had made it a policy that we were going to interrogate these guys harshly.

[The actual standard was] 'we're not going to follow the Geneva Conventions but we are going to treat you humanely.' Well, what does humane mean? To me humane means I can kind of play with your mind, but I cannot hit you or do anything that is going to cost you permanent physical damage. To [another officer I spoke with] humane means it's okay to rough someone up and to do physical harm. Not to break bones or anything like that but to do physical harm as long as you're not humiliating him, which was the way he put it. We've got people with different views of what humane means and there's no Army statement that says this is the standard for humane treatment for prisoners to Army officers. Army officers are left to come up with their own definition of humane treatment.

I don't know for sure [how high up the hierarchy responsibility for the abusive treatment lies]. What I know is that it's widespread enough that it's an officer problem. It's at least an officer problem. You make the standard, and that is what goes up to the executive branch. You communicate the standard, that's when it's somewhat the executive branch, but then it comes more into the officer branch, and enforcing the standard is the officer branch ... And in the Schlesinger report [of August 2004, into detainee abuse by US forces] it even says that when the President made the decision that al-Qaeda wasn't going to be covered by the Geneva Conventions, there was a clear danger that it was going to undermine the culture in the United States Army that enforces strict adherence to the law of land warfare. That's in the Schlesinger report.

But anyway, the President makes that decision, and decides that we're not going to cover them by the Geneva Conventions, which according to the letter of the law, I think there's a strong argument for that.... [But] then that lack of standard migrates throughout the Army. It filters throughout the Army, so that now the standard, this convoluted, 'You'll know what's right when you see it,' filters through the whole Army.

If you draw a hard line and you say 'Don't do anything bad to prisoners,' like you bring them in, you give them food, you give them water, and then you leave them alone. If that happens then, yeah, that is an easy line to draw, but when you start drawing shades of grey and you start stripping prisoners, or you start making prisoners do humiliating things and then you tell a soldier to draw the line somewhere, then no. A soldier is not going to be able to draw that line because as soon as you cross that line and as soon as you start stripping prisoners or you start making people do vigorous exercise, or you start basically putting yourself in a position of authority where you are subjecting someone else to harsh treatment, things are going to get out of hand because everyone is going to draw the line at a different place. Just like the discussion between me and the other officer, where's the line? What is acceptable and what is not acceptable? People don't know. The West Point officers knew the line coming out of West Point. We knew where the Geneva Conventions drew the line, but then you get that confusion when the Secretary of Defence and the President make that statement. And we were confused.

[In Iraq, my understanding of how we should treat prisoners] didn't change. There are a couple of reasons for that. Pre-deployment training was minimal going to Iraq because we deployed on short notice from West Point through Fort Bragg to Iraq. So there might be some disconnect there, but also none of the unit policies changed. Iraq was cast as part of the War on Terror, not a separate entity in and of itself, but a part of a larger war.

[I didn't discuss abuse of detainees with my superiors in Iraq because] to me, it was obviously part of the system and the reasons had been laid out about why we're not following the Geneva Conventions in respect to the detainees. We did follow them in other aspects and once that was laid out I thought it was pretty clear cut ... That was just the way I thought we were running things.

Another officer approached me and was like 'I'm not sure this is the way you should be treating someone.' It was almost like an off-hand, kind of like...just a conversation like making a comment. He said something like 'I don't know if this is right' and my response was 'Hey, it's out in the open and we've said that we are doing this. It's not like we're doing it on the sly.'

If I as an officer think we're not even following the Geneva Conventions, there's something wrong. If officers witness all these things happening, and don't take action, there's something wrong. If another West Pointer tells me he thinks, 'Well, hitting somebody might be okay,' there's something wrong.

What I'm saying is had I thought we were following the Geneva Conventions as an officer I would have investigated what was clearly a very suspicious situation.

Implications of the Abu Ghraib abuse revelations

Someone mentioned to me in passing that there was a really bad prisoner abuse scandal and I took note of it and I thought, 'that is horrible. That is going to be bad public relations for the Army' and I thought, 'Okay, rogues did something.' And then as the week progressed I watched on the news and they showed some of the pictures – not all of them – a large portion of the pictures were in accordance with what I perceived as US policy. Now all the stuff with sodomy with the chem light and all that was clearly beyond what I would have allowed to happen on a personal moral level and what I thought policy was. But the other stuff, guys handcuffed naked to cells in uncomfortable positions, guys placed in stress positions on boxes, people stripped naked. All that was ... If I would have seen it, I would have thought it was in accordance with interrogation procedures...

The first concern when this originally happened was loyalty to the Constitution and separation of powers, and combined with that is the honour code: 'I will not lie, cheat or steal or tolerate those who do.' The fact that it was systematic, and that the chain of command knew about it was so obvious to me that [until that point] I didn't even consider the fact that other factors might be at play, so that's why I approached my chain of command about it right off the bat and said, 'Hey, we're lying right now. We need to be completely honest.'

Congress should have oversight of treatment of prisoners. That is the way; the Army should not take it upon itself to determine what is acceptable for America to do in regards to treatment of prisoners. That's a value ... that's more than just a military decision, that's a values decision, and therefore Congress needs to know about it, and therefore the American people need to have an honest representation of what's going on presented to them so that they can have a say in that.

The failure of the officer corps

It's unjust to hold only lower-ranking soldiers accountable for something that is so clearly, at a minimum, an officer corps problem, and probably a combination with the executive branch of government.

It's almost infuriating to me. It is infuriating to me that officers are not lined up to accept responsibility for what happened. It blows my mind that officers are not. It should've started with the chain of command at Abu Ghraib and anybody else that witnessed anything that violated the Geneva Conventions, or anything that could be questionable should've been standing up saying, 'This is what happened. This is why I allowed it to happen. This is my responsibility,' for the reasons I mentioned before. That's basic officership, that's what you learn at West Point, that's what you should learn at any commissioning source ...

Look, the guys who did this aren't dishonourable men. It's not like they are a bunch of vagabonds. They've shown more courage and done more things in the time that I've spent with them than I could cover in probably a week of talking to you. They are just amazing men, but they're human. If you put them in a situation, which is the officer's responsibility, where they are put in charge of somebody who tried to kill them or maybe killed their friend, bad things are going to happen. It's the officer's job to make sure bad things don't happen.

[Another important] thing is making sure this doesn't happen again...[We need] to address the fact that it was an officer issue and by trying to claim that it was 'rogue elements' we seriously hinder our ability to ensure this doesn't happen again. And, that has not only moral consequences, but it has practical consequences in our ability to wage the War on Terror. We're mounting a counter-insurgency campaign, and if we have widespread violations of the Geneva Conventions, that seriously undermines our ability to win the hearts and minds of the Muslim world.

[I]f America holds something as the moral standard, it should be unacceptable for us as a people to change that moral standard based on fear. The measure of a person or a people's character is not what they do when everything is comfortable. It's what they do in an extremely trying and difficult situation, and if we want to claim that these are our ideals and our values then we need to hold to them no matter how dark the situation.

The role of the 'Other Governmental Agency'

In Afghanistan we were attached to Special Forces and saw OGA ('Other Governmental Agency' – a term that is frequently used to refer to the CIA). We never interacted with them but they would stress guys. We learned how to do it. We saw it when we would guard an interrogation.

They [OGA interrogators in Afghanistan] had a horn. In this case they would involve US soldiers. There was a really loud horn and any time the detainee would fall asleep they would blare the horn in his ear so that he had to wake up and they would do that until he stood up again and stayed awake.

[A]t Forward Operating Base Tiger [near the Syrian border] there were a lot of high value targets and ... there was a Special Forces team nearby, and I was going to talk to them just about career stuff and as I was going out I saw someone who I thought was Other Governmental Agency ... go into the prisoner detainee holding facility and take one of the detainees out. And then they took infantry guards and they went into an unoccupied building that they could seal off, closed the door, and they gave orders to the infantry guards not to let anyone in. The reason I know this is because I was trying to talk to the Special Forces guys and I asked them 'Hey, do you know where the SF guys are?' and they were like 'Well, maybe some of them are in here but you can't go in there right now. They are with a prisoner.' And there were noises coming out of there. There could have been physical violence but [they were at least] threatening the prisoner ... doing things that weren't actually causing bodily harm but threatening to do that.

I talked to a Military Policeman who said that he was in charge of holding detainees and that the CIA would just come and take the detainees away. They would be like, 'How many detainees do you have?' and he knew he has seventeen detainees but the OGA would be like, 'No, you have sixteen,' so he'd be like 'Alright. I have sixteen.' And who knows where that detainee went.

**Extraordinary Rendition
The new interrogators**
Case Study VI

Privatised Interrogation

Pratap Chatterjee

Dozens of people converged this summer in the high desert town of El Paso, Texas, en route to spending six months in Iraqi prisons. They were going not as prisoners, but as their interrogators, walking a legalistic tightrope stretched across the Geneva Conventions. Just for signing up, they got a $2,000 check from a company that is rapidly becoming one of the key employers in the world of intelligence: Lockheed Martin, the world's biggest military company, based in Bethesda, Maryland.

Before deployment to Iraq, they assemble in Building 503 on Pleasanton Road to mingle with the soldiers and government civilian workers at the welcome briefing that takes place every Sunday. There they get a government-issued duffel bag, filled with basic items for working in the war in the Middle East: cargo pants, tactical shirts, Kevlar helmets and Land Warrior chemical masks. After a week of orientation and medical processing, they fly to Tampa, Florida, and onto their final work destinations – Iraq's infamous prisons including Abu Ghraib, Camp Cropper, a prison at Baghdad International Airport, and Camp Whitehorse, near Nasariyah.

Known in the intelligence community as '97 Echoes' (97E is the official classification number for the interrogator course taught at military colleges including Fort Huachuca, Arizona), these contractors will work side-by-side with military interrogators conducting question-and-answer sessions using 17 officially sanctioned techniques, ranging from 'love of comrades' to 'fear up harsh.' Their subjects will be the tens of thousands of men thrown into United States-run military jails on suspicion of links to terrorism.

The rules that govern all interrogators, both contract and military, are currently open to broad interpretation. Today there is much legal wrangling about where to draw the line between harsh treatment and torture. An amendment to the latest military spending bill introduced by

Pratap Chatterjee is the managing editor and project director of CorpWatch (www.corpwatch.org). He is the author of Iraq Inc., A Profitable Occupation *(Seven Stories Press).*

Senator John McCain, an Arizona Republican, explicitly bars the use of torture on anyone in United States custody. His amendment was approved by 90 to 9 votes in the United States Senate. McCain was fighting off Vice President Dick Cheney's suggestion that Central Intelligence Agency counter-terrorism agents working overseas be exempted from the torture ban.

Jobs for this new breed of interrogators typically begin with a phone call or e-mail to retired Lieutenant Colonel Marc Michaelis, in the quaint old flour milling town of Ellicott City, on the banks of the Patapsco River in Maryland, about an hour's drive from Washington DC. Michaelis, who is the main point of contact for new interrogators, came to Lockheed in February after it acquired his former employer Sytex in a $462 million takeover. Sytex was founded in 1988 by Sydney Martin, a management graduate of the Massachusetts Institute of Technology who dabbles in collecting old Danish and Irish coins. In its first year, the Pennsylvania-based company earned $1,500. By 2004, according to Congressional Quarterly, Sytex was providing 'personnel and technology solutions to government customers including the Pentagon's Northern Command, the Army's Intelligence and Security Command, and the Department of Homeland Security.' Its revenues had reached $425 million.

The bottom line was undoubtedly improved by the boom in hiring contract interrogators that began just weeks after the September 11, 2001 attacks on the World Trade Centre in New York. Armed with new Pentagon contracts, Michaelis advertised job openings for 120 new 'intelligence analysts' ranging from Arab linguists to counter-intelligence and information warfare specialists. The private contractors would work at Fort Belvoir, Virginia, and at the United States Special Operations Command in Tampa, Florida.

At the same time, Lockheed Martin, then a completely different company, was also interested in entering this lucrative new business of intelligence contracting. It bought up Affiliated Computer Services (ACS), a small company with a General Services Administration (GSA) technology contract issued in Kansas City, Missouri. In November 2002, Lockheed used General Services Administration to employ private interrogators at Guantánamo Bay, Cuba. The contract was then transferred to a Department of Interior office in Sierra Vista, Arizona.

The issue of private contractors in interrogation did not come to light until mid-2004, when a military investigation revealed that several interrogators at the Abu Ghraib prison were civilian employees of CACI (formerly Consolidated Analysis Centers, Inc). The contract to the Virginia-based company was also issued by the Department of Interior's Sierra Vista, Arizona office, located a stone's throw from the headquarters of the Army's main interrogation school.

(CACI did not actually bid on the original contract, but like Lockheed in Guantánamo, it had bought another company – Premier Technology Group – which did. The Fairfax, Virginia-based firm provided interrogators to the Pentagon in August 2003 under a General Services Administration contract for information technology services.)

One of the interrogators, Steven Stefanowicz, was accused of involvement in the Abu Ghraib prison torture scandal that broke in May 2004. It was soon revealed that Stefanowicz, who was trained as a satellite image analyst, had received no formal training in military interrogation, which involves instruction in the Geneva Conventions on human rights.

A subsequent report in July 2004, by Lieutenant General Paul Mikolashek, on behalf of the Army Inspector General, found that a third of the interrogators supplied in Iraq by CACI had not been trained in military interrogation methods and policies. The same report mentioned that of the four contract interrogators employed by Sytex in Bagram, Afghanistan, only two had received military interrogation training, and the other two, who were former police officers, had not.

It also emerged that no one knew what laws applied to private contractors who engaged in torture in Iraq, or whether they were in fact accountable to any legal authority or disciplinary procedures. When the media began to question the role of the private contractors and the legality of their presence under unrelated information technology contracts from non-military agencies, the Pentagon swiftly issued sole-source ('no bid') military contracts to CACI and Lockheed.

That CACI contract expired at the end of September 2005. But before the company opted not to renew its contract, the company was already working with Sytex as a sub-contractor to supply new personnel to interrogate prisoners.

No new contractor in either Iraq or Afghanistan has been officially announced to date, but Major Matthew McLaughlin, a spokesperson for United States Central Command at MacDill Air Force Base in Tampa, Florida, told CorpWatch: 'The Army is the executive agent for contracting all interrogator type services for the Department of Defence. They work their contracts (writ large) from an office which operates out of Fort Belvoir, Virginia.'

Sytex, and thus Lockheed after the takeover, appears to have subsequently emerged as one of the biggest recruiters of private interrogators. In June alone, Sytex advertised for 11 new interrogators for Iraq, and in July the company sought 23 interrogators for Afghanistan. It has also been seeking experienced report writers and programme managers who have worked in military interrogations in Operation Iraqi Freedom, Operation Enduring Freedom, former Yugoslavia, or the Persian Gulf War.

Advertisements on several websites frequented by current and former military personnel offered a $70,000 to $90,000 salary, a $2,000 sign-up bonus, $1,000 for a mid-tour break, and a $2,000 bonus for completing the normal six month deployment. Those returning for a second tour get double bonuses at the beginning and end of their stints. In return, the employees are expected to work as necessary – up to 14 hours a day, 7 days a week. (The companies, however, get to bill the military up to $200 an hour for this work, according to Cherif Bassiouni, the former United Nations Independent Expert on the Situation of Human Rights in Afghanistan.)

'Sytex is one of our best customers,' says Bill Golden, a former military intelligence analyst with 20 years Army experience, who now runs IntelligenceCareers.com, one of the biggest intelligence employment websites in the business. 'They are the main company hiring 97E workers today.'

Golden attributes the current boom in private contract interrogators to poor military planning over the last decade. 'The military worked as hard as it could to create a brain drain by moving qualified intelligence people into other jobs, who then quit. As a result by September 11, 2001, there was no one left who had a clue. Now they are rushing to catch up and create 9,000 new specialists, but it takes at least five years to become really experienced. What we have now is a nursery full of babies in the army.'

Yet even by 2003, just 237 new interrogators were graduated from the intelligence school at Fort Huachuca. Today, a Virginia-based company, Anteon, has contracted with the base to provide private instructors to increase the number of qualified interrogators completing intelligence courses to 1,000 a year in 2006.

The scope of contracts for companies like Anteon and Sytex are difficult to determine because they have never been made public. Asked about the details of the interrogation contracts, Lockheed declined to comment. Joseph Wagovich, a spokesman for the company's information technology division that includes Sytex, initially told CorpWatch that the company had only a minor role in the interrogation business and that the company had wrapped up its interrogation contract on Guantánamo. But he confirmed that Lockheed was still supplying other kinds of 'intelligence analysts' on the Cuban base.

Sytex itself also likes to keep a low profile. 'Most of the law enforcement organisations, as well as the other surreptitious organisations we may be supporting, would just as soon not see their names in print,' Ralph Palmieri Junior, the company's Chief Operating Officer, told Congressional Quarterly in 2004.

Even without all the specifics, it is clear that Lockheed is supplying the US war in Iraq with a vast range of both personnel and *matériel*. In addition to providing interrogators, it is currently seeking retired Army majors or lieutenant colonels to develop short- and long-range planning at the biggest US base in Iraq: Camp Anaconda, in Balad, northern Iraq. Also being courted for work in Iraq are 'red switch' experts to run the military's secure communications systems.

On the *matériel* side, Lockheed's Keyhole and Lacrosse satellites beam images from the war back to the military; its U-2 and the SR-71 Blackbird spy planes, F-16, F/A-22 jet fighters, and F-117 stealth attack fighters were used to 'shock and awe' the Iraqis at the start of the US invasion; and ground troops employed its Hellfire air-to-ground missiles and the Javelin portable missiles in the invasion of Fallujah last year.

The company's reach and influence go far beyond the military. A *New York Times* profile of the company in 2004 opened with the sentence: 'Lockheed Martin doesn't run the United States. But it does help run a breathtakingly big part of it.' 'Over the last decade, Lockheed, the nation's largest military contractor, has built a formidable information-technology empire that now stretches from the Pentagon to the Post Office. It sorts your mail and totals your taxes. It cuts Social Security checks and counts the United States census. It runs space flights and monitors air traffic. To make all that happen, Lockheed writes more computer code than Microsoft,' writes Tim Weiner.

The national security reporter for *The New York Times* explains how Lockheed gets its business: 'Men who have worked, lobbied and lawyered for Lockheed hold the posts of secretary of the Navy, secretary of transportation, director of the national nuclear weapons complex, and director of the national spy satellite agency.'

'Giving one company this much power in matters of war and peace is as dangerous as it is undemocratic,' says Bill Hartung, senior fellow at the World Policy Institute in New York. 'Lockheed Martin is now positioned to profit from every level of the war on terror from targeting to intervention, and from occupation to interrogation.

Apart from the monopoly on war-related contracts to one single corporation, the increased outsourcing of interrogation to private contractors raises questions of accountability and of enforcement of regulations designed for the military.

Human rights groups are openly critical of this new trend. 'The Army's use of contract interrogators has to date been a failed experiment,' Deborah Pearlstein told CorpWatch. 'Based on the Pentagon's own investigations and other reports that are already public, it seems clear that contractors are less well trained, less well controlled, and harder to hold accountable for things that go wrong than are regular troops.' Pearlstein, who is the director of the US Law and Security Program at Human Rights First (formerly Lawyers Committee on Human Rights), warned that 'unless and until contract interrogators can be brought at the very least up to the standards of training and discipline expected of our uniformed soldiers, the United States may well be better off without their services.'

Former interrogators have a more nuanced opinion. 'The problem is not the use of civilian contractors,' one former Army interrogator with over ten years of field experience, wrote in an e-mail to CorpWatch. 'What is necessary is an active means of supervision and oversight on ALL of our assets in the field... not just the civilian ones. If you take a look at many of the investigations of the military intelligence activities, you will find just as many uniformed individuals breaking the law as contractors. I am more interested in providing proper guidance, training, supervision and oversight to ALL of our intelligence people.'

But Susan Burke, a lawyer for Iraqi prisoners who say they were tortured at Abu Ghraib, challenges the legality of using private contractors for interrogation. 'Interrogation has always been considered an inherently governmental function for obvious reasons. It is irresponsible and dangerous to use contractors in such settings given that there is a long history of repeated human rights abuses by contractors.' The Philadephia attorney charges that the use of private contractors is illegal. 'The United States Congress has passed laws (the Federal Acquisition Regulations) that prevent the executive branch from delegating "inherently governmental functions" to private parties.'

'The US does not condone...'

*Condoleezza Rice
Andrew Tyrie MP*

On 5 December 2005, before visiting Europe, United States Secretary of State Condoleezza Rice tried to rebutt persistent complaints that the US transported detainees to countries practising torture, and that some of these 'extraordinary renditions' took place via Europe. We reprint Ms Rice's statement in full. We also feature a commentary on this statement by Andrew Tyrie MP.

'We have received inquiries from the European Union, the Council of Europe, and from several individual countries about media reports concerning US conduct in the war on terror. I am going to respond now to those inquiries, as I depart today for Europe. And this will also essentially form the text of the letter that I will send to Secretary Straw, who wrote on behalf of the European Union as the European Union President.

The United States and many other countries are waging a war against terrorism. For our country this war often takes the form of conventional military operations in places like Afghanistan and Iraq. Sometimes this is a political struggle, a war of ideas. It is a struggle waged also by our law enforcement agencies. Often we engage the enemy through the cooperation of our intelligence services with their foreign counterparts.

We must track down terrorists who seek refuge in areas where governments cannot take effective action, including where the terrorists cannot in practice be reached by the ordinary processes of law. In such places terrorists have planned the killings of thousands of innocents – in New York City or Nairobi, in Bali or London, in Madrid or Beslan, in Casablanca or Istanbul. Just two weeks ago I also visited a hotel ballroom in Amman, viewing the silent, shattered aftermath of one of those attacks.

The United States, and those countries that share the commitment to defend their citizens, will use every lawful weapon to defeat these terrorists. Protecting citizens is the first and oldest duty of any government. Sometimes these efforts are misunderstood. I want to help all of you understand the hard choices involved, and some of the responsibilities that go with them.

One of the difficult issues in this new kind of conflict is what to do with captured individuals who we know or believe to be terrorists. The individuals come from many countries and are often captured far from their original homes. Among them are those who are effectively stateless, owing allegiance only to the extremist cause of transnational terrorism. Many are extremely dangerous. And some have information that may save lives, perhaps even thousands of lives.

The captured terrorists of the 21st century do not fit easily into traditional systems of criminal or military justice, which were designed for different needs. We have to adapt. Other governments are now also facing this challenge.

We consider the captured members of al Qaeda and its affiliates to be unlawful combatants who may be held, in accordance with the law of war, to keep them from killing innocents. We must treat them in accordance with our laws, which reflect the values of the American people. We must question them to gather potentially significant, life-saving, intelligence. We must bring terrorists to justice wherever possible.

For decades, the United States and other countries have used 'renditions' to transport terrorist suspects from the country where they were captured to their home country or to other countries where they can be questioned, held, or brought to justice.

In some situations a terrorist suspect can be extradited according to traditional judicial procedures. But there have long been many other cases where, for some reason, the local government cannot detain or prosecute a suspect, and traditional extradition is not a good option. In those cases the local government can make the sovereign choice to cooperate in a rendition. Such renditions are permissible under international law and are consistent with the responsibilities of those governments to protect their citizens.

Rendition is a vital tool in combating transnational terrorism. Its use is not unique to the United States, or to the current administration. Last year, then Director of Central Intelligence George Tenet recalled that our earlier counterterrorism successes included 'the rendition of many dozens of terrorists prior to September 11, 2001.'

– Ramzi Youssef masterminded the 1993 bombing of the World Trade Centre and plotted to blow up airlines over the Pacific Ocean, killing a Japanese airline passenger in a test of one of his bombs. Once tracked down, a rendition brought him to the United States, where he now serves a life sentence.

– One of history's most infamous terrorists, best known as 'Carlos the Jackal,' had participated in murders in Europe and the Middle East. He was finally captured in Sudan in 1994. A rendition by the French government brought him to justice in France, where he is now imprisoned. Indeed, the European Commission of Human Rights rejected Carlos' claim that his rendition from Sudan was unlawful.

Renditions take terrorists out of action, and save lives.

In conducting such renditions, it is the policy of the United States, and I presume of any other democracies who use this procedure, to comply with its laws and comply with its treaty obligations, including those under the Convention Against Torture. Torture is a term that is defined by law. We rely on our law to govern our operations. The United States does not permit, tolerate, or condone torture under any

circumstances. Moreover, in accordance with the policy of this administration:
- The United States has respected – and will continue to respect – the sovereignty of other countries.
- The United States does not transport, and has not transported, detainees from one country to another for the purpose of interrogation using torture.
- The United States does not use the airspace or the airports of any country for the purpose of transporting a detainee to a country where he or she will be tortured.
- The United States has not transported anyone, and will not transport anyone, to a country when we believe he will be tortured. Where appropriate, the United States seeks assurances that transferred persons will not be tortured.

International law allows a state to detain enemy combatants for the duration of hostilities. Detainees may only be held for an extended period if the intelligence or other evidence against them has been carefully evaluated and supports a determination that detention is lawful. The US does not seek to hold anyone for a period beyond what is necessary to evaluate the intelligence or other evidence against them, prevent further acts of terrorism, or hold them for legal proceedings.

With respect to detainees, the United States Government complies with its Constitution, its laws, and its treaty obligations. Acts of physical or mental torture are expressly prohibited. The United States Government does not authorise or condone torture of detainees. Torture, and conspiracy to commit torture, are crimes under US law, wherever they may occur in the world.

Violations of these and other detention standards have been investigated and punished. There have been cases of unlawful treatment of detainees, such as the abuse of a detainee by an intelligence agency contractor in Afghanistan or the horrible mistreatment of some prisoners at Abu Ghraib that sickened us all and which arose under the different legal framework that applies to armed conflict in Iraq. In such cases the United States has vigorously investigated, and where appropriate, prosecuted and punished those responsible. Some individuals have already been sentenced to lengthy terms in prison; others have been demoted or reprimanded.

As CIA Director Goss recently stated, our intelligence agencies have handled the gathering of intelligence from a very small number of extremely dangerous detainees, including the individuals who planned the 9/11 attacks in the United States, the attack on the USS *Cole*, and many other murders and attempted murders. It is the policy of the United States that this questioning is to be conducted within US law and treaty obligations, without using torture. It is also US policy that authorised interrogation will be consistent with US obligations under the Convention Against Torture, which prohibit cruel, inhuman, or degrading treatment. The intelligence so gathered has stopped terrorist attacks and saved innocent lives – in Europe as well as in the United States and other countries. The United States has fully respected the sovereignty of other countries that cooperate in these matters.

Because this war on terrorism challenges traditional norms and precedents of previous conflicts, our citizens have been discussing and debating the proper legal standards that should apply. President Bush is working with the US Congress to

come up with good solutions. I want to emphasise a few key points.
- The United States is a country of laws. My colleagues and I have sworn to support and defend the Constitution of the United States. We believe in the rule of law.
- The United States Government must protect its citizens. We and our friends around the world have the responsibility to work together in finding practical ways to defend ourselves against ruthless enemies. And these terrorists are some of the most ruthless enemies we face.
- We cannot discuss information that would compromise the success of intelligence, law enforcement, and military operations. We expect that other nations share this view.

Some governments choose to cooperate with the United States in intelligence, law enforcement, or military matters. That cooperation is a two-way street. We share intelligence that has helped protect European countries from attack, helping save European lives.

It is up to those governments and their citizens to decide if they wish to work with us to prevent terrorist attacks against their own country or other countries,

---

Are we being misled?

'"We're operating under our laws, we're operating under our international obligations," is the refrain. But these cleverly crafted words do not mean what they appear to say. The US position is premised on the claim that its actions comply with US law and, since US law complies with its international obligations, these too are being complied with. The claim is flawed.

Take the definition of torture. The definitions under the 1984 torture convention and the relevant US statute are not the same. The threshold for torture is lower under international law: acts that do not amount to torture under US law may do so under international law. "Waterboarding" – strapping a detainee to a board and dunking him under water so he believes that he might drown – plainly constitutes torture under international law, even if it may not do so under US law.

How, then, does the administration justify the claim that US law trumps? When the US joined the 1984 convention it entered an "understanding" on the definition of torture, to the effect that the international definition was to be read as being consistent with the US definition. The administration relies on the "understanding". So, when Condoleezza Rice says the US does not do torture or render people to countries that practise torture, she does not rely on the international definition. That is wrong: the convention does not allow each country to adopt its own definition, otherwise the convention's obligations would become meaningless. That is why other governments believe the US "understanding" cannot affect US obligations under the convention. They are right.'

Philippe Sands, Financial Times,
9 December 2005

and decide how much sensitive information they can make public. They have a sovereign right to make that choice.

Debate in and among democracies is natural and healthy. I hope that that debate also includes a healthy regard for the responsibilities of governments to protect their citizens.

Four years after September 11, most of our populations are asking us if we are doing all that we can to protect them. I know what it is like to face an inquiry into whether everything was done that could have been done. So now, before the next attack, we should all consider the hard choices that democratic governments must face. And we can all best meet this danger if we work together.'

* * *

Assurances from Jack Straw and Condoleezza Rice over torture flights are 'as good as worthless'

On 13th December 2005, the All Party Parliamentary Group on Extraordinary Rendition at Westminster published a legal Opinion commissioned from leading authority James Crawford, Whewell Professor of International Law at the University of Cambridge.

The Opinion shows that the United Kingdom may not be fulfilling its legal obligations, despite Jack Straw's protestations to the contrary.

The opinion analyses the statement made by United States Secretary of State Condoleezza Rice on 5th December in response to allegations that the United States is engaging in unlawful renditions of terror suspects. It also advises on the legal issues related to the concern that United Kingdom territory or facilities may have been used to assist the US in carrying out 'torture flights'.

Andrew Tyrie MP, Chairman of the All Party Parliamentary Group, said:

> 'Jack Straw said on the Today programme: "careful research has been unable to identify any occasion... when we have received a request for permission by the United States for a rendition through the UK territory or airspace... [the Foreign and Commonwealth Office] have found no records."
>
> This should reassure nobody.
>
> On the specific issue of records, on the 13th July the Home Office told me in an answer to a Parliamentary Question (Number 442 27.6.05): "records of a transit application are not kept once the transit has been completed." So it's hardly surprising there are no records.'

Mr Tyrie continued:

> 'It is crystal clear that the United Kingdom must investigate allegations that it has been complicit in torture. Checking for instances of the US requesting permission is simply derisory.
>
> Two important conclusions come from Professor Crawford's Opinion. First, to comply with its legal obligation the British government must satisfy itself that Extraordinary Rendition is not leading to torture. As Professor Crawford puts it: "the question that must be asked is whether torture is likely to take place if a person is transported, irrespective of whether or not the government claims that the answer is no, or what its hopes or beliefs may be" (para. 20).

Secondly, relying on Condoleezza Rice's assurance provides little or no legal cover for the government. Condoleezza Rice's assurance is based on the US government's interpretation of its obligations but they are as good as worthless for ensuring compliance with Britain's legal obligations. It is the duty of the UK government to take all the necessary active steps to achieve this.

In particular, as Professor Crawford clarifies, all UK assistance to US aircraft which may be engaged in Extraordinary Rendition should be conditional on the United States respecting obligations not to engage in torture, at the legal standard at which the obligations apply to the United Kingdom. In other words, if the US is to use UK airports and airspace for these practices, the United States must abide by the legal rules that bind the United Kingdom and UK courts' interpretation of them, not just US law or the US administration's interpretation of them.

We also need a thorough investigation of detailed allegations that have been made.[1]

For example, the Saad Madni case raises a number of specific questions which Mr Straw needs to answer:

> Did this Gulfstream 5 stop in the UK?
> Was Mr Madni on board?
> Did the United States seek permission for this flight to refuel?
> Did the United Kingdom give permission for the flight to refuel?
> Was Mr Madni likely to be tortured as a result of this transfer?'

Mr Tyrie concluded:

'Professor Crawford is not raising abstract legal or technical issues. His opinion goes to the heart of what's being done in our name. There should be no place for torture in British Foreign Policy, nor for turning a blind eye to it.

The government's position is now badly exposed. Jack Straw knows this very well. That is why he has been engaging in the same sort of legally inspired economy with the truth that we have already seen from Condoleezza Rice.

The truth will come out on all of this eventually, anyway. It would be far better for Britain's standing in the world, and for the government, if it told us now.

If many people's concerns and fears turn out to be well grounded, we will be undermining the very values that we are seeking to export and, as a result, we will make ourselves less secure not more.'

The All Party Parliamentary Group on Extraordinary Rendition is chaired by Andrew Tyrie MP. It is a cross party group and comprises over 50 MPs and Peers.

Reference

1. In the case of Saad Iqbal Madni, it was alleged that: The Gulfstream V on to which Iqbal was bundled and flown to Egypt left Cairo on January 15 [2002] and headed for Scotland. After a brief stopover at Prestwick, probably to refuel, it departed again for Washington. Iqbal was held in Cairo for two years before appearing in Guantánamo, where he told other detainees who have since been released that he was tortured by having electrodes placed on his knees. It also appears that his bladder was damaged during interrogation. See 'Destination Cairo: human rights fears over CIA flights'. Ian Cobain, Stephen Grey, Richard Norton Taylor. *The Guardian*, September 12 2005.

American Prisoners in Europe

Human Rights Watch

Dick Marty

Council of Europe

Human Rights Watch, a non-governmental organisation, has urged the United Nations and relevant European Union bodies to launch investigations to determine which countries have been or are being used by the United States for transiting and detaining incommunicado prisoners.

Dick Marty of the Council of Europe's Legal Affairs Committee reports on the key aspects of his inquiry regarding the alleged existence of secret detention centres in Council of Europe member states and flights which may have transferred prisoners without any judicial involvement.

I

The *Washington Post* reported on 3 November 2005 that the United States has used secret detention facilities in Eastern Europe and elsewhere to illegally hold terrorist suspects without rights or access to counsel. Citing US government concerns, the article did not identify the locations in Eastern Europe.

Human Rights Watch has conducted independent research on the existence of secret detention locations that corroborates the *Washington Post's* allegations that there were detention facilities in Eastern Europe. Specifically, we have collected information that CIA airplanes travelling from Afghanistan in 2003 and 2004 made direct flights to remote airfields in Poland and Romania. Human Rights Watch has viewed flight records showing that a Boeing 737, registration number N313P – a plane that the CIA used to move several prisoners to and from Europe, Afghanistan, and the Middle East in 2003 and 2004 – landed in Poland and Romania on direct flights from Afghanistan on two occasions in 2003 and 2004. Human Rights Watch has independently confirmed several parts of the flight records, and supplemented the records with independent research.

According to the records, the N313P plane flew from Kabul to north-east Poland on 22 September 2003, specifically, to Szymany airport, near the Polish town of Szczytno, in Warmia-Mazuria province. Human Rights Watch has obtained information that several detainees who had been held secretly in Afghanistan in 2003 were transferred out of the country in September and October 2003. The Polish intelligence service maintains a large training facility and grounds near the Szymany airport.

The records show that the N313P plane landed the next day, 23 September 2003, at the Mihail Kogalniceanu military airfield in Romania. The flight records indicate that the plane flew on to Morocco the same day, and then to Guantánamo Bay. The Department of

Defence, which releases information about all detainee transfers to Guantánamo, released no statement about a transfer to Guantánamo around this date.

According to our research, the United States has been using the Mihail Kogalniceanu airfield in Romania for operations in Iraq and Afghanistan since 2002, and the base has been closed to the public and journalists since early 2004. Secretary of Defence Donald Rumsfeld visited Romania and the Mihail Kogalniceanu base in October 2004. The N313P plane also flew from Kabul to Timisoara airport in Romania on January 25, 2004.

The Associated Press quoted Szymany airport officials in Poland confirming that a Boeing passenger plane landed at the airport at around midnight on the night of September 22, 2003. The officials stated that the plane spent an hour on the ground and took aboard five passengers with US passports.

The N313P airplane, and other planes allegedly used by the CIA to transport prisoners, have also repeatedly landed at airports in Jordan, Morocco, Egypt, and Libya, as well as in Germany, the United Kingdom, Switzerland, Spain, Portugal, Macedonia, Cyprus, the Czech Republic, and Greece. Most of these landings have taken place at major civilian airports or joint civilian-military airports, both unlikely locales for clandestine operations. The Szymany and Mihail Kogalniceanu airfields are more remote.

Further investigation is needed to determine the possible involvement of Poland and Romania in the extremely serious activities described in the *Washington Post* article. Arbitrary incommunicado detention is illegal under international law. It often acts as a foundation for torture and mistreatment of detainees. US government officials, speaking anonymously to journalists in the past, have admitted that some secretly held detainees have been subjected to torture and other mistreatment, including waterboarding (immersing or smothering a detainee with water until he believes he is about to drown). Countries that allow secret detention programmes to operate on their territory are complicit in the human rights abuses committed against detainees.

Human Rights Watch knows the names of 23 high-level suspects being held secretly by US personnel at undisclosed locations. An unknown number of other detainees may be held at the request of the US government in locations in the Middle East and Asia. US intelligence officials, speaking anonymously to journalists, have stated that approximately 100 persons are being held in secret detention abroad by the United States.

Human Rights Watch emphasises that there is no doubt that secret detention facilities operated by the United States exist. The Bush Administration has cited, in speeches and in public documents, arrests of several terrorist suspects now held in unknown locations. Some of the detainees cited by the administration include: Abu Zubaydah, a Palestinian arrested in Pakistan in March 2002; Ramzi bin al-Shibh, arrested in September 2002; Abd al-Rahim al-Nashiri (also known as Abu Bilal al-Makki), arrested in United Arab Emirates in November 2002; Khalid Sheikh Mohammed, arrested in Pakistan in March 2003 along with Mustafa al-Hawsawi; and Hambali (aka Riduan Isamuddin) arrested in Thailand in August 2003.

Human Rights Watch urges the United Nations and relevant European Union bodies to launch investigations to determine which countries have been or are being used by the United States for transiting and detaining incommunicado prisoners. The US Congress should also convene hearings on the allegations and demand that the Bush administration account for secret detainees, explain the legal basis for their continued detention, and make arrangements to screen detainees to determine their legal status under domestic and international law. We welcome the decision by the Legal Affairs Committee of the Parliamentary Assembly of the Council of Europe to examine the existence of US-run detention centres in Council of Europe member states (see below). We also urge the European Union, including the EU Counter-Terrorism Coordinator, to further investigate allegations and publish its findings.

* * *

II
Council of Europe investigates CIA flights

At the meeting of the Parliamentary Assembly of the Council of Europe's Committee on Legal Affairs and Human Rights held in Paris on 13 December 2005, the rapporteur and Chair of the Committee, Dick Marty, reported on the key aspects of his inquiry regarding the alleged existence of secret detention centres in Council of Europe member states and flights which may have transferred prisoners without any judicial involvement. He said the following steps had been taken.

Letters had been sent to the delegations to the Parliamentary Assembly of the two countries explicitly mentioned in the media, namely Poland and Romania, and to the Permanent Observer of the United States to the Council of Europe (the Romanian Delegation replied on 17 November 2005, while the Permanent Observer of the United States had sent him a copy of a speech made by Ms Condoleezza Rice, US Secretary of State, on 5 December 2005 [see page 64]; to date, the Polish delegation had not replied).

Letters requesting detailed information had been sent to the Director General of Eurocontrol [European Organisation for the Safety of Air Navigation] and the Director of the European Union Satellite Centre (EUSC). In an interim reply, the Eurocontrol Director had indicated that he first had to obtain the necessary authorisation to make an exception to the usual data protection rules, while the Deputy Director of the Satellite Centre had indicated that supplying images of the kind requested by Mr Marty was not part of the centre's usual remit. The Committee on Legal Affairs therefore called on the Council of the European Union (and Mr Javier Solana, Secretary General of the Council of the European Union and High Representative of the European Union for the Common Foreign and Security Policy) to intercede with the Satellite Centre so that progress could be made here and urged the European Commission and the member states of Eurocontrol to ensure that its executive body grant authorisation for the transmission of the data requested.

The rapporteur had made direct contacts with non-governmental organisations, in particular Human Rights Watch, while Parliamentary Assembly President René van der Linden had also been in contact with a number of individuals concerned (including an exchange of letters with Ms Rice); the rapporteur had also exchanged information with investigative journalists.

The rapporteur welcomed the opening by the Secretary General of the Council of Europe of the procedure under Article 52 of the European Convention on Human Rights for the purpose of obtaining relevant information from all contracting parties to the convention. He also expressed particular satisfaction at the willingness of Mr Franco Frattini, Vice-President of the European Commission, to co-operate closely with the Council of Europe on the matter. In this connection, he welcomed the participation of a representative of the European Commission and a member of the European Parliament at today's meeting.

From a general point of view, the rapporteur underlined that the information gathered to date reinforced the credibility of the allegations concerning the transfer and temporary detention of individuals, without any judicial involvement, in European countries.

Legal proceedings in progress in certain countries seemed to indicate that individuals had been abducted and transferred to other countries without respect for any legal standards. It had to be noted that the allegations had never been formally denied by the United States. The rapporteur takes note of the situation and deplores the fact that no information or explanations had been provided on this point by Ms Rice during her visit to Europe.

The rapporteur urges all member governments to commit themselves fully to establishing the truth about flights over their territories in recent years by aeroplanes carrying individuals arrested and detained without any judicial involvement. The rapporteur intends to ask the leaders of the parliamentary delegations to the Assembly to take initiatives within their parliaments in order to obtain more precise information on this matter, either by putting questions to their governments or by proposing the setting up of committees of inquiry. In fact, the delegations to the Parliamentary Assembly can make use of their unique position to lobby national parliaments to shed light on the matter. Mr Marty welcomes the fact that steps have already been taken here by certain national parliaments.

Postscript: On 15 January 2006, a Swiss newspaper, *Sonntags Blik*, published an intercepted fax between the Egyptian Foreign Ministry and its London Embassy which was sent in November 2005. This reveals that the Egyptians had learned through intelligence contacts that the CIA had interrogated 23 Iraqi and Afghan citizens in the secret Mihail Kogalniceanu prison, near the Romanian city of Constanza on the Black Sea. It also indicates that similar interrogation centres are situated in the Ukraine, Bulgaria, Kosovo, and Macedonia.

Precedents for Torture

Naomi Klein

Naomi Klein is the author of No Logo. *She wrote and produced* The Take*, a documentary film about Argentina's occupied factories. Her essay on 'The Rise of Disaster Capitalism' was published in Spokesman 85 (*Apocalypse Soon*). With grateful acknowledgements to* The Nation.
© *Naomi Klien*

It was the 'Mission Accomplished' of George Bush's second term, and an announcement of that magnitude called for a suitably dramatic location. But what was the right backdrop for the infamous 'We do not torture' declaration? With characteristic audacity, the Bush team settled on downtown Panama City.

It was certainly bold. An hour and a half's drive from where Bush stood, the US military ran the notorious School of the Americas from 1946 to 1984, a sinister educational institution that, if it had a motto, might have been 'We do torture'. It is here in Panama, and later at the school's new location in Fort Benning, Georgia, where the roots of the current torture scandals can be found.

According to declassified training manuals, School of the Americas students – military and police officers from across the hemisphere – were instructed in many of the same 'coercive interrogation' techniques that have since gone to Guantánamo and Abu Ghraib: early morning capture to maximise shock, immediate hooding and blindfolding, forced nudity, sensory deprivation, sensory overload, sleep and food 'manipulation', humiliation, extreme temperatures, isolation, stress positions – and worse. In 1996, President Clinton's Intelligence Oversight Board admitted that US-produced training materials condoned 'execution of guerrillas, extortion, physical abuse, coercion and false imprisonment'.

Some Panama school graduates went on to commit the continent's greatest war crimes of the past half-century: the murders of Archbishop Oscar Romero and six Jesuit priests in El Salvador; the systematic theft of babies from Argentina's 'disappeared' prisoners; the massacre of 900 civilians in El Mozote in El Salvador; and military coups too numerous to list here.

Yet when covering the Bush announcement, not a single mainstream news outlet mentioned the location's sordid history. How could they?

That would require something totally absent from the debate: an admission that the embrace of torture by US officials has been integral to US foreign policy since the Vietnam war.

It's a history exhaustively documented in an avalanche of books, declassified documents, CIA training manuals, court records and truth commissions. In his forthcoming book, *A Question of Torture*, Alfred McCoy synthesises this evidence, producing a riveting account of how monstrous CIA-funded experiments on psychiatric patients and prisoners in the 1950s turned into a template for what he calls 'no-touch torture', based on sensory deprivation and self-inflicted pain. McCoy traces how these methods were field-tested by CIA agents in Vietnam as part of the Phoenix programme and then imported to Latin America and Asia under the guise of police training.

It is not only apologists for torture who ignore this history when they blame abuses on 'a few bad apples'. A startling number of torture's most prominent opponents keep telling us that the idea of torturing prisoners first occurred to US officials on 11 September 2001, at which point the methods used in Guantánamo apparently emerged, fully formed, from the sadistic recesses of Dick Cheney's and Donald Rumsfeld's brains. Up until that moment, we are told, America fought its enemies while keeping its humanity intact.

The principal propagator of this narrative (what Garry Wills termed 'original sinlessness') is Senator John McCain. Writing in *Newsweek* on the need to ban torture, McCain says that when he was a prisoner of war in Hanoi, he held fast to the knowledge 'that we were different from our enemies ... that we, if the roles were reversed, would not disgrace ourselves by committing or approving such mistreatment of them'. It is a stunning historical distortion. By the time McCain was taken captive, the CIA had launched the Phoenix programme and, as McCoy writes, 'its agents were operating 40 interrogation centres in South Vietnam that killed more than 20,000 suspects and tortured thousands more.'

Does it somehow lessen today's horrors to admit that this is not the first time the US government has used torture, that it has operated secret prisons before, that it has actively supported regimes that tried to erase the left by dropping students out of airplanes? That, closer to home, photographs of lynchings were traded and sold as trophies and warnings? Many seem to think so. On November 8, Democratic Congressman Jim McDermott made the astonishing claim to the House of Representatives that 'America has never had a question about its moral integrity, until now'.

Other cultures deal with a legacy of torture by declaring 'Never again!' Why do so many Americans insist on dealing with the current torture crisis by crying 'Never before'? I suspect it stems from a sincere desire to convey the seriousness of this administration's crimes. And its open embrace of torture is indeed unprecedented.

But let's be clear about what is unprecedented: not the torture, but the openness. Past administrations kept their 'black ops' secret; the crimes were sanctioned but they were committed in the shadows, officially denied and condemned. The Bush administration has broken this deal: post-9/11, it demanded the right to torture without shame, legitimised by new definitions and new laws.

Despite all the talk of outsourced torture, the real innovation has been insourcing, with prisoners being abused by US citizens in US-run prisons and transported to third countries in US planes. It is this departure from clandestine etiquette that has so much of the military and intelligence community up in arms: Bush has robbed everyone of plausible deniability. This shift is of huge significance. When torture is covertly practised but officially and legally repudiated, there is still hope that if atrocities are exposed, justice could prevail. When torture is pseudo-legal and those responsible deny that it is torture, what dies is what Hannah Arendt called 'the juridical person in man'. Soon victims no longer bother to search for justice, so sure are they of the futility, and danger, of that quest. This is a larger mirror of what happens inside the torture chamber, when prisoners are told they can scream all they want because no one can hear them and no one is going to save them.

In Latin America the revelations of US torture in Iraq have not been met with shock and disbelief but with powerful *déjà vu* and reawakened fears. Hector Mondragon, a Colombian activist who was tortured in the 1970s by an officer trained at the School of the Americas, wrote: 'It was hard to see the photos of the torture in Iraq because I too was tortured. I saw myself naked with my feet fastened together and my hands tied behind my back. I saw my own head covered with a cloth bag. I remembered my feelings – the humiliation, pain.' Dianna Ortiz, an American nun who was brutally tortured in a Guatemalan jail, said, 'I could not even stand to look at those photographs... so many of the things in the photographs had also been done to me. I was tortured with a frightening dog and also rats. And they were always filming.'

Ortiz has testified that the men who raped her and burned her with cigarettes more than 100 times deferred to a man who spoke Spanish with an American accent whom they called 'Boss.' It is one of many stories told by prisoners in Latin America of mysterious English-speaking men walking in and out of their torture cells, proposing questions, offering tips. Several of these cases are documented in Jennifer Harbury's powerful new book, *Truth, Torture, and the American Way*.

Some of the countries that were mauled by US-sponsored torture regimes have tried to repair their social fabric through truth commissions and war crimes trials. In most cases, justice has been elusive, but past abuses have been entered into the official record and entire societies have asked themselves questions not only about individual responsibility but collective complicity. The United States, though an active participant in these 'dirty wars,' has gone through no parallel process of national soul-searching.

The result is that the memory of US complicity in far-away crimes remains fragile, living on in old newspaper articles, out-of-print books and tenacious grassroots initiatives like the annual protests outside the School of the Americas (which has been renamed but remains largely unchanged). The terrible irony of the anti-historicism of the torture debate is that in the name of eradicating future abuses, these past crimes are being erased from the record. Every time Americans repeat the fairy tale about their pre-Cheney innocence, these already hazy memories fade even further. The hard evidence still exists, of course, carefully archived in the tens of thousands of declassified documents available from the National Security Archive. But inside US collective memory, the disappeared are being disappeared all over again.

This casual amnesia does a disservice not only to the victims of these crimes, but also to the cause of trying to remove torture from the US policy arsenal once and for all. Already there are signs that the administration will deal with the uproar by returning to plausible deniability. The McCain amendment protects every 'individual in the custody or under the physical control of the United States government'; it says nothing about torture training or buying information from the exploding industry of for-profit interrogators.

And in Iraq the dirty work is already being handed over to Iraqi death squads, trained by the US and supervised by commanders like Jim Steele, who prepared for the job by setting up similar units in El Salvador. The US role in training and supervising Iraq's interior ministry was forgotten, moreover, when 173 prisoners were recently discovered in a ministry dungeon, some tortured so badly that their skin was falling off. 'Look, it's a sovereign country. The Iraqi government exists,' Rumsfeld said. He sounded just like the CIA's William Colby who, asked in a 1971 Congressional probe about the thousands killed under Phoenix, a programme he helped launch, replied that it was now 'entirely a South Vietnamese programme'.

And that's the problem with pretending that the Bush Administration invented torture. 'If you don't understand the history and the depths of the institutional and public complicity,' says McCoy, 'then you can't begin to undertake meaningful reforms.' Lawmakers will respond to pressure by eliminating one small piece of the torture apparatus: closing a prison, shutting down a programme, even demanding the resignation of a really bad apple like Rumsfeld. But, McCoy says, 'they will preserve the prerogative to torture.'

Rendition is Abduction

Lord Steyn interviewed by Jon Snow

In November 2003, Lord Steyn's described Guantánamo Bay as a 'legal black hole' (see Spokesman 81). He was then a senior English judge (Lord of Appeal in Ordinary), and his remarks attracted wide attention. He gave this interview to Jon Snow of Channel 4 News in December 2005. We are publishing it with the agreement of Channel 4 to make it more widely avilable.

Jon Snow: *Lord Steyn, when asked to talk about the whole question of torture, about rendition, the US Secretary of State said that the captured terrorists of the 21st Century do not fit easily into the traditional system of criminal, military justice. Isn't it a reality that what is happening is a response to a kind of human behaviour that international law isn't used to having to deal with?*

Lord Steyn: It is undoubtedly from 9/11 onwards a new situation, and modern terrorism involves far greater risks to the public. But, in my view, it is even more important now that one must stand by human rights law, respect the treaties. The need for them has not been lessened, but increased.

Jon Snow: *The Americans are saying that European lives have been saved by carrying people from one place to another. They deny torture.*

Lord Steyn: I can't see that that is a proposition that can be sustained. Specifically when you refer to torture it is very important to know what is meant by torture. I'm speaking purely as a lawyer. The US administration has adopted a definition of torture which is extremely narrow. It involves causing death, total organ failure and so forth. The true definition is much wider and it includes coercive questioning.

Jon Snow: *Do you therefore think that in a way Guantánamo Bay is a template for what is happening?*

Lord Steyn: I think Guantánamo Bay is the clue to much of what we have seen unravelled. We have seen a scale of lawlessness unravel which in my opinion is the logical extension of Guantánamo Bay because Guantánamo Bay involved taking prisoners from Afghanistan, and many other places, to an island where there would be a lawless black hole where they can never escape from, where they have no right to trial. This logically is not very different from what the Americans call rendition, which, in truth, is abduction. It is not authorised by international law and the connection between this and Guatánamo Bay is very close.

Jon Snow: *So you use the phrase lawlessness of states behaviour. A very strong phrase and when counterbalanced with, say, the scene in Israel yesterday, when five civilians were killed by a suicide bomber, who's the lawless party?*

Lord Steyn: Of course everybody condemns terrorism – it's a scourge, an outrage. But we do not improve the modern world or make it safer by adopting methods that have outraged a very large part of the world. They've outraged the devout Muslim world, the moderate Muslim world. It is just simply a fact that events for example like Abu Ghraib would have outraged moderate Muslims throughout the world.

Jon Snow: *Let's leave aside the question of torture which in a sense you've dealt with. Is it legal to move people around the world from one detention centre to another?*

Lord Steyn: It is undoubtedly not legal. One must go back to the Geneva Convention and the matter is governed by the Geneva Conventions and prisoners must be dealt with in accordance with the Geneva Conventions. And the Geneva Convention is not something you can opt into or opt out as you like. Those are binding conventions.

Jon Snow: *Don't you accept the American's view that these are not prisoners of war but merely illegal combatants?*

Lord Steyn: No. The argument that they are illegal combatants because they didn't wear uniforms is not one a court would find terribly impressive. So I wouldn't accept that. But in any event, if the Geneva Conventions are not binding then customary international law is of the same effect, and the United States is undoubtedly bound by customary international law.

Jon Snow: *But you'd accept that there's obviously a conflict about whether this is legal or not? Even the British Government has gone some way to saying what is happening is legal.*

Lord Steyn: It is true that the British Government has said through the Defence Secretary that what the Americans are doing in Guatánamo Bay is legal, but that is a very surprising thing for the British Government to have said. I have a copy here or what the Defence Secretary said. Mr Hoon said: 'There is no doubting the legality in the way these combatants have been imprisoned.' He added: 'There is no doubting the legality of the US to move them for trial.' That's at Guantánamo Bay. That's a very surprising thing for the British Government to have said, and I'm not sure the British Government would want that to be repeated today.

Jon Snow: *But if your position is right, how is it that the international legal system has so totally failed when it comes to Guantánamo, which is now nearly four years old?*

Lord Steyn: That is true, of course. Guantánamo Bay went straight up to the US Supreme Court and the Supreme Court appeared to give decisions in favour of the detainees, but a couple of months ago there was a decision to the effect that it was lawful to try these prisoners by military commissions on the island. And now the matter is going back to the US Supreme Court, and we're all in limbo four years later.

Jon Snow: *The question of black sites, the question of not declaring where these people are being held – why is that not accepted by international law if the politicians in the system are saying; 'Look, this is defending innocent lives from assault by people who want to kill them'?*

Lord Steyn: The answer to that is relatively straightforward. International law consists of treaties, and in this particular case the relevant treaties are the Geneva Conventions, and they govern the position of people who are detained, and the detainees must be treated in accordance with that law. But that is buttressed, strengthened too, by customary international law, which is largely to the same effect. Now that is binding law. That's not something someone can opt in or opt out as one chooses – it is binding law that binds the United States and it binds the United Kingdom Government.

Jon Snow: *But as things stand, it is law that is being broken in your terms. What is the cumulative effect then of Guantánamo, of removal and of black sites?*

Lord Steyn: The cumulative effect of all these matters is lawlessness on a truly grand scale. It has the effect of giving a setback to international law, to humanitarian law – human rights law – for a very, very long time. And what was built up after the Second World War ensured an international rule of law. I'm specifically referring to Nuremberg, to the United Nations Charter, the Universal Declaration of Human Rights, the international covenants. I'm referring to things like Pinochet, the creation of the International Criminal Court, all those events are hugely damaged by what has been done here.

Jon Snow: *What about those countries that allow these things to happen?*

Lord Steyn: As far as that is concerned, we can go back to Nuremberg. The person who tortures, who beats up prisoners, can be guilty of torture depending on the level pain that is inflicted. But it doesn't end there. The person who authorises someone to do the beating may be guilty of torture and of a war crime. And what's more, somebody who set up a system calculated to cause such events to take place himself could be guilty of war crimes.

Jon Snow: *But the very concept of a war crime is an enormous statement. You are actually saying people who are doing this at the moment may be guilty of a war crime?*

Lord Steyn: If prisoners are tortured at Guantánamo Bay or at black sites – if they are – those who commit those acts will be guilty of war crimes, and those who authorise it can be similarly guilty of war crime.

Jon Snow: *Does the landing of the plane, does the knowledge of passage of an individual through your country perhaps destined for mistreatment, amount to a war crime?*

Lord Steyn: It's going to depend on degree. But once there is knowledge of the detainees may be tortured, there is a risk that those who facilitate these flights may be guilty.

Jon Snow: *Let me press you then, the British authorities may be guilty of war crimes?*

Lord Steyn: If the British authorities were fully aware of the purpose of the flights. If they were aware that these were attempts to take detainees to places where they could be tortured, of course there is the risk that the British authorities may themselves be guilty of war crimes. But it is dependent of proof.

Jon Snow: *What do you say to the civil power who says; 'We are confronted by a threat to our citizens from the suicide bomber which is without precedent, we have to adapt. And your system of international law isn't adapting fast enough'?*

Lord Steyn: I give the answer that President Barak, the president of the Israeli Supreme Court – and a very outstanding lawyer – has given to that. The answer he gives is that a democracy must sometimes fight with his hands tied behind his back. And that way it becomes stronger, not weaker.

Jon Snow: *What then do we ask of our government from a legal perspective?*

Lord Steyn: From a legal perspective, I would say we are at least entitled to ask of our government that it must stand up to the international rule of law, that it must do so unambiguously and publicly. That necessarily involves that there should be no kow-towing to the lawlessness of the US administration.

Who Fooled America?

Lawrence Wilkerson

On 29th November 2005, the BBC Today Programme broadcast Caroline Quinn's interview with Colonel Lawrence Wilkerson, former Chief of Staff to the US Secretary of State, Colin Powell.

LW The post-invasion planning for Iraq was handled, in my opinion, in this alternative decision-making process, which in this case constituted the Vice President, the Secretary of Defence and certain people in the Defence Department who did the 'post-invasion planning' which was as inept and incompetent as any planning anyone has ever done. It consisted of largely sending Jay Garner and his organisation to sit in Kuwait until the military forces had moved into Baghdad, and then going to Baghdad and other places in Iraq with no other purpose than to deliver a little humanitarian assistance, perhaps deal with some oilfield fires, put Ahmed Chalabi or some other similar Iraqi in charge, and leave. This was not only inept and incompetent, it was daydreaming of the most unfortunate type, and ever since that failed we've been in a pick-up game that's costs us over 2000 Americans killed in action, and almost a Division's worth of casualties.

BBC You call this alternative decision-making as a process. You seem to be laying the blame pretty squarely at the door of Dick Cheney. Am I correct in assuming that?

LW In the two decision-making processes into which I had the most insight, the detainee abuse issue, and this issue of post-invasion planning for Iraq, I lay the blame squarely at his feet. I look at the relationship between Mr Cheney and Mr Rumsfeld as being one that produced these two failures in particular. And I see that the President is not holding either of them accountable, or at least up to this point he is not. And so I have to lay some blame at his feet, too.

BBC You are talking about the abuse, alleged abuse by American forces, aren't you?

LW I am. And I concluded that we had had an impassioned debate in the statutory process, and in that debate two sides had participated. One that essentially wanted to do away with all restrictions, and the other which said 'no, Geneva should prevail', and the President walked right down the middle. He made a decision that Geneva would, in fact, govern all but al Qaeda and al Qaeda look-alike detainees. Any other prisoners would be governed by traditional methods, international law, Geneva and so forth.

BBC Who was calling for doing away with all the normal practices, if you like?

LW Who is right now, very publicly, lobbying the Congress of the United States advocating the use of terror – the Vice President of the United States.

BBC There was a presidential memo ordering that detainees be treated in a manner consistent with the Geneva Conventions that forbid torture. Are you saying that Dick Cheney ordered that to be ignored?

LW My critics have said that the President's continuing phrase in what you just quoted, 'consistent with military necessity', was an out, under which almost anything could be done. If I'm a soldier in the field, an NCO, a private or a corporal, and I need to shoot even a detainee who might be threatening to kill one of my buddies, or even me, I can do that. It does not mean that I can go into a darkened cell with the detainee shackled with his hands above his head, to the wall, and beat him, so that eventually he dies and the Army Coroner declares it homicide. And two years later, when the Army quits obfuscating, and throwing obstacles in the way of the investigations, people are actually punished for having murdered two individuals in Bagram, Afghanistan in December 2002. And there were more than seventy such deaths, questionable deaths of detainees, under US supervision when I left the State Department. And I have people now telling me that the death toll is up to around ninety.

BBC The question of detainee abuse. Are you saying that the implicit message allowing it to happen was sanctioned by Dick Cheney? It came from his office?

LW You see two sides of this debate in the statutory process. You see the side represented by Colin Powell, Will Taft, all arguing for Geneva. You see the other side represented by John Yoo from the Department of Justice, Alberto Gonzales, you see the other side being argued by them, and the President compromising. Then you see the Secretary of Defence moving out in his own memorandum to act as if the side that declared everything open, free, and anything goes actually being what's implemented. And so what I'm saying is under the Vice President's protection, the Secretary of Defence moved out to do what they wanted to do in the first place even though the President had made a decision that was clearly a compromise.

BBC It's quite difficult to believe that Colin Powell wasn't aware of what was going on, that this alternative decision-making process was going on. Why didn't he do something?

LW You don't know that it's happening.

BBC If what you say is correct, in your view is Dick Cheney then guilty of a war crime?

LW That's an interesting question. It was certainly a domestic crime to advocate terror. And I would suspect that it is, for whatever it's worth, an international crime as well.

BBC You've got also John Kerry recently accusing President Bush of orchestrating one of the great acts of deception in American history and saying that flawed intelligence was manipulated to fit a political agenda. Colin Powell would be tarred with that same brush, wouldn't he? Did he feel that he had correct information about Iraq's alleged weapons of mass destruction when he outlined the case against Saddam?

LW He certainly did. And so did I. I was intimately involved in that process, and to this point I have more or less defended the administration. I have basically been supportive of the administration's point that it was simply fooled, that the intelligence community, including the UK, Germany, France, Jordan, other countries that confirmed what we had in our intelligence package, that we were all just fooled. Lately, I'm growing increasingly concerned because two things have just happened here that really made me wonder. One is the questioning of Sheikh Al Libi* where his confessions were obtained through interrogation techniques other than those authorised by Geneva. It led Colin Powell to say at the UN on 5 February 2003 that there were some pretty substantive contacts between al Qaeda and Baghdad. We now know that Al Libi's forced confession has been recanted, and we know, we are pretty sure that it was invalid. More important than that, we know that there is a Defence Intelligence Agency dissent on that testimony, even before Colin Powell made his presentation. We never heard about that. Follow that up with Curveball, and the fact that the Germans now say that they told our CIA well before Colin Powell gave his presentation, that Curveball, the source for the biological mobile laboratories, was lying, and was not a trustworthy source, and then you begin to speculate, you begin to wonder was this intelligence spun, was it politicised, was it cherry picked? Did, in fact, the American people get fooled? I'm beginning to have my concerns.

---

*The New York Times subsequently reported (8 December 2005) that Mr Ali Libi made his most specific claims linking al Qaeda to Iraq after the United States handed him over to interrogators in Egypt.

THE BERTRAND RUSSELL PEACE FOUNDATION
DOSSIER

ISRAEL'S QUEST FOR HEAVY WATER – AN UPDATE

In *Spokesman 88* we reported how, in 1959, Britain aided the proliferation of nuclear weapons to the Middle East by shipping the first consignment of 20 tons of heavy water to Israel for use in its new nuclear reactor at Dimona. Britain had originally obtained the heavy water from Norway. Now, the Norwegian Ministry of Foreign Affairs has for the first time published some of the key documents about the sale to Israel.

The documents show that, in May 1958, Israel asked to buy 20 tons of heavy water through the Norwegian company Noratom. Heavy water is used in certain types of nuclear reactors where it acts as a moderator to slow down neutrons so that they can react with the uranium. It is regarded as the cheap way to build an atomic bomb. At this time, only Norway and the United States could supply heavy water in these quantities. American heavy water was half the price of Norwegian, but was subject to rigid controls which would have prevented Israel from using it to produce atomic weapons.

Long before the negotiations for the purchase had started, the Norwegian Ministry of Foreign Affairs received secret communiqués from both Sweden and Canada. These said that both countries had received requests from Israel to participate in the production of atomic weapons, together with Israel and France. This collaboration would be completely independent of the United States. Norwegian Foreign Minister Hans Engen was informed of these approaches in a secret note dated 13th January 1959 – a month before the sale agreement was signed. The note relates that Israel had invited Canada and Sweden to participate in the production of nuclear weapons. Both countries already had there own programmes for the development of nuclear weapons. Israel's requests were a clear indication of the real motivation behind its nuclear programme – to build its own arsenal of nuclear weapons. Even so, the Norwegian Foreign Ministry did not prevent the sale. Israel had to sign an agreement that the heavy water was only to be used for peaceful purposes, and that Norway had the right to inspect to ensure that this promise was kept. Norway carried out only one such inspection, in 1961, after pressure from the United States. Two years later, the Dimona reactor started up.

But what was the role of the British Government in this sale? Officially, the heavy water was sold back to Noratom, the Norwegian state-owned company, from where it had come in the first place. But the British Government did this knowing that Noratom would immediately sell on the 20 tons of heavy water to Israel. In fact, it was collected directly from a British port by Israeli ships.

After BBC Newsnight originally broadcast the story in August 2005, the Arab League wrote to the International Atomic Energy Agency seeking a full investigation. British Foreign Office minister Kim Howells subsequently told Mohamed ElBaradei, Director General of the Agency, that Britain did not sell the material to Israel. 'The United Kingdom was not in fact a party to the sale of heavy water to Israel,' he wrote, 'but did negotiate the sale back to Norway of surplus heavy water.' Britain then circulated that response to every International Atomic Energy Agency member government.

BBC Newsnight has now tracked down Donald Cape, one of the Foreign Office officials involved in deciding that British heavy water should be shipped to Israel. In September 1958, Cape received a letter in which the United Kingdom Atomic Energy Authority admitted: 'It could be argued that the Israelis will receive the heavy water by reason of our reselling it to Noratom; that therefore we are parties to the supply to Israel.' In fact, Israel's contract with Noratom says Noratom would provide heavy water from the United Kingdom Atomic Energy Authority for Israel – delivered in Britain to Israel. Noratom would take a commission of two per cent on the four million dollar deal; its responsibility would be 'limited' to that of 'consultant'.

Confidential letters obtained by Newsnight through a Freedom of Information request, written two months before the first delivery was collected by Israel, show the British Foreign Office knew Israel had secretly tried to buy uranium from South Africa – without safeguards. One letter quotes secret CIA reports from 1957 and 1958, which took the view that 'The Israelis must be expected to try and establish a nuclear weapons programme as soon as the means were available to them.' The man who wrote these Foreign Office letters was Donald Cape himself.

When the existence of the Israel's nuclear reactor at Dimona was revealed to the world in December 1960, British intelligence made an assessment of Israeli capabilities. These minutes are really the only occasion on which the British Government has ever released a detailed assessment of Israel's nuclear weapons programme, and they show just how important Britain's 20 tons of heavy water were to that programme. According to the Joint Intelligence Assessment, it meant that the Dimona reactor would be able to make enough plutonium to build up to six atom bombs a year. The document concludes: 'It has been, and remains our opinion, that Israel wanted an independent supply of plutonium so as to be in a position to make nuclear weapons if she wished.' Yet the Foreign Office imposed no restrictions on what the heavy water would be used for.

With grateful acknowledgements to the Norwegian Peace Alliance which supplied information about the Norwegian Foreign Ministry documents.

EVADING THE INTERNATIONAL CRIMINAL COURT

The United States is the only state that has been actively campaigning against the International Criminal Court. The Bush Administration has repeatedly voiced fears that the Court could be used to bring politically motivated prosecutions against US nationals. On that basis it is demanding that governments around the world sign impunity agreements to prevent them from surrendering US nationals accused of genocide, crimes against humanity and war crimes to the Court.

However, the Bush administration has run into increasing criticism in the US Congress as needlessly antagonising friendly countries. In addition, in a significant retreat from its previous opposition to other states ratifying the Rome Statute of the Court, it stated in the United Nations General Assembly on 23 November 2005 that '[w]e respect the right of other states to become parties to the Rome Statute; we ask in return, however, that other states respect our decision not to do so.'

Amnesty International has analysed the bilateral impunity agreements which the United States has entered into with more than 80 governments and has concluded that they are illegal. They violate both the Rome Statute and other conventions under international law – including the Geneva Conventions and the Convention against Torture and Other Cruel, Inhuman or Degrading Treatment or Punishment – all of which demand that persons responsible for the crimes are brought to justice. The European Union has analysed these agreements and reached the same conclusion.

Despite threats by the United States to withdraw 'economic support funds' and military assistance to countries that refuse to sign impunity agreements, more than 50 countries have committed to uphold the fundamental principle that no one can have impunity for these crimes by refusing to sign. They include European Union states, Argentina, Brazil, Canada, Japan, Mali, Mexico, New Zealand, Paraguay, Peru, Samoa, Slovenia, South Africa, St. Lucia, Switzerland, Tanzania, Trinidad and Tobago, Uruguay and Venezuela.

According to the *New York Times*, Niger is also amongst the countries that have refused to enter into a 'bilateral immunity agreement' with the United States. It says its Constitution does not allow it to grant the immunity agreement. So the Bush administration is cutting off certain support funds. Yet Niger is the poorest country in the world, according to the United Nations, where one in four children die before the age of five. Many of them die in the repeated famines which afflict the country, as we have seen all too plainly in recent months.

To date, more than 80 states have reportedly entered into impunity agreements with the United States. In most states, the agreement has been signed by the government. The agreement then requires approval by Parliament to be ratified before it becomes legally binding. According to reports, parliaments in Sierra Leone, Georgia, Honduras, Bosnia-Herzegovina, Albania, Gambia, Mauritania, Azerbaijan, Nicaragua, Panama, Tajikistan, Macedonia, Guyana, Kazakhstan,

Ghana, El Salvador, Bhutan, Timor-Leste and Mozambique have ratified such agreements. In other cases, when governments have signed impunity agreements, national parliaments are refusing to ratify them.

Sources: www.amnesty.org, www.nytimes.com

WHAT HAPPENED IN GREECE?

'... let me just say in respect of those allegations that they are complete nonsense and no United Kingdom officials have taken part in any alleged mistreatment in Greece of any suspects whatsoever and we were not involved in the arrest or detention of those particular suspects.'

Jack Straw, 13 December 2005,
in response to questions at the Foreign Affairs Committee

On 7 July 2005, four bombs were exploded on three tube trains and a bus in London. Fifty-six people died, including four bombers, and many more were injured. In Greece, ten days later, 28 Pakistani workers were detained by the Greek secret service, apparently with the involvement of members of British Secret Intelligence Service.

The Pakistanis, who were migrant workers in Greece, say that as they were abducted their shirts were pulled over their heads so that they could not see, and that they were beaten and threatened with guns. They were held for several days. During their interrogation, they were asked about their involvement in the London bombings. Relatives in Pakistan were also detained at the same time and questioned about the bombings. The Pakistanis said that two British personnel, one of whom was 'dark-skinned', were present during some of the interrogations.

The Greek journal *Proto Thema* has named fifteen Greeks and one Briton as participating in the abduction and detention of the Pakistanis. *Proto Thema* also claims that the Greek Prime Minister, Kostas Karamanlis, sanctioned the British-led operation. It named two officials working in his office as taking part in the negotiations over the incident.

Some of the Pakistanis are now bringing a legal action in Greece against their Greek abductors. Lawyers representing them have filed a complaint against the agents named by the Greek newspaper report. 'We have accused them of abduction and torture,' said Frangiskos Ragoussis, their lawyer. 'We will also request that they produce any documents – especially tapes – recording the interrogations.'

The Greek government has announced an inquiry, and the chief prosecutor in Athens, Dimitris Papangelopoulos, has asked that the case be made over from the police to the prosecutor's office.

Munir Mohamed, one of the Pakistanis who were abducted, said that when they finally let him go, they told him, 'Don't you dare tell a word about what happened in here. If we find out you said something, either we'll bring you here again or we'll cut your throat'. Mr Mohamed also said that the questions they asked him were about an old friend who used to live in London, with whom he hadn't any contact for at least six months. When asked why they waited for some months before publicising their accusations, Mr Mohamed said: 'When your life is threatened, you don't want to speak, even to your father, about it'.

Alekos Alavanos, the leader of Greece's opposition Coalition of the Left party, said of the UK government: 'They have to say if British services were involved in this act, that is against the democratic traditions of Europe, against the laws of human rights of the European Union, against the laws on torture of the UN, against the constitutions of every democratic country in Europe.'

TERRORISM BILL – 'WORRYING PRECEDENT'

Louise Arbour, the United Nations High Commissioner for Human Rights, sent two special investigators to Britain in 2004. Following their visit, she wrote to the British Government to warn that key parts of its new Terrorism Bill would set worrying precedents. The Bill seeks to outlaw incitement to terrorism and would extend the period suspects can be held without charge.

In her letter, Ms Arbour wrote:

> 'Parts of this Bill could pose grave challenges to effective human rights protection and set worrying precedents in the global struggle against terrorism. I believe that the Bill would benefit from further scrutiny to ensure that its provisions are in conformity with international and regional standards.'

She specified particular concerns:
- There is no precise definition of terrorism; phrases such as 'encouragement of terrorism' are too 'broad and sweeping';
- People could be found guilty of disseminating terrorist publications without 'actual intent';
- The proposed crime of glorifying terrorism 'fails to strike a balance between security considerations and the fundamental right of free expression';
- Grounds for proscribing groups that encourage terrorism are 'too broad';
- She was 'gravely concerned' about extending detention without charge from 14 to 28 days.

The British Government ignored Ms Arbour's plea to raise her warnings in time for the House of Lords to consider them before completing their discussion of the Bill on 20 December 2005. Even though Ms Arbour sent her letter on 28 November, Charles Clarke, the Home Secretary, did not make it available to Parliamentarians until 9 January 2005.

Reviews

The Neocons: Seymour's Antidote

Seymour M. Hersh, *Chain of Command*, Penguin, 432 pages, 2005, paperback ISBN 0141020881, £7.99

Seymour Hersh has been for some years providing in *The New York Times*, *The New Yorker* and elsewhere the inside story of the takeover of the Bush administration, US military and intelligence services by a group of neoconservatives, Vice President Dick Cheney, Donald Rumsfeld, Paul Wolfowitz, Richard Perle and John Bolton in particular. One of the most important results of this takeover, as Hersh has revealed it, is how through a top secret Presidential order called the 'Special-Access Programme' (SAP), the Defence Department was authorised to recruit a clandestine team of special forces operatives to carry out a 'manhunt' for al Qaeda all over the world and outside of international law. What we have learnt of the obscenities at Guantánamo Bay and at Abu Graibh prison in Iraq have not been the result of a few individuals acting on their own initiative, but part of a 'chain of command' going back to the very top. Yet, while eight enlisted men and women have been charged, no officer or higher authority is facing criminal proceedings for the treatment of prisoners. The very man who had been in command of Guantánamo, Major General Geoffrey Miller, was sent to take charge of Abu Graibh.

Hersh starts by dealing with the ambiguity over the definition of torture, which has led US officials, including Condoleezza Rice, to deny all accusations that the US authorities were condoning the use of torture. Rice's words on the subject are interesting: 'The Administration can't overthrow the whole detention and interrogation facility.' Hersh's most important point is that all the interrogations and use of special forces have dismally failed to produce any crucial intelligence, just as all the US intelligence systems failed to reveal that Saddam Hussein had no weapons of mass destruction, or to anticipate the bombings of 9/11, in spite of warnings from other countries' intelligence services. What emerges from Hersh's revelations is the quite extraordinary degree of rivalry and non-cooperation between the different branches of the US military and civilian intelligence.

On the results of the war in Afghanistan, Hersh quotes Hy Rothstein, a retired army colonel who was charged by the Defence Department's Office of Special Operations and Low Intensity Conflict to examine the planning and execution of the war. 'The conditions under which the post-Taliban government came to power gave [in Rothstein's words] "warlordism, banditry and opium production a new lease on life".' Opium production, which had fallen to 185 metric tons in a year under the Taliban, had, according to a UN report of 2003, soared to 3,600 tons. On the position of women, Judy Benjamin, who was the gender adviser to the US Agency for International Development, is quoted by Hersh telling him, 'The legal opportunities have improved but the day to day life for women, even in Kabul, isn't any better.'

Hersh's revelations about the decision of what he calls the 'Iraq hawks' to go to war in Iraq some time before 2003 are now well known, but he is able to quote a former US National Security Council staff member saying, 'As of February 2002, the decision to go to war was taken'. One of the leading hawks, Richard Perle, his role as chairman of the Defence Policy Board and the conflict with his interest in arms and oil in Saudi Arabia, are fully examined by Hersh who concludes, 'There is no question that Perle believed that removing Saddam from power was the right thing to do. At the same time, he set up a company that stood to gain from a war ...' Ahmad Chalabi's role as leader of the Iraqi National Congress and the US nominee for the premiership after the war is described in detail by Hersh, with all the evidence that Chalabi was responsible for feeding the Americans with stories of Saddam's supposed weapons of mass destruction and of a supposed likely uprising in Iraq in support of a US liberating force.

The role of the special forces of the US Defence Department was much enhanced once the invasion of Iraq had begun. This was all part of Rumsfeld's faith in a small military ground force supported heavily from the air (secret forces which would also not be counted in the total). The one-time Ba'athist leadership under Saddam was to be eliminated by 'preemptive manhunting' starting with Saddam himself and the top 50 members of the leadership, some to be held for interrogation, others apparently to be assassinated. Lt.General William G. Boykin was brought back from retirement by Rumsfeld to plan the manhunt offensive. Boykin was reported by *The Los Angeles Times* to have spoken to US church groups 'repeatedly equating the Muslim world with Satan.' Hersh points out that the manhunt created a body of 'tens of thousands of unemployed former military officers and enlistees ... who plot, plan ... and at night go out on their missions', their motivation being nationalist and their target the US 'occupation', as they saw it. Far from fighting terrorism in Iraq, the Americans have in fact been generating it among the Iraqis with a modicum of help from al Qaeda.

A penultimate chapter is devoted by Hersh to General Pervez Musharraf, the President of Pakistan, whom Hersh describes as a 'most dangerous friend' of the US President. The duplicity of Musharraf arises from the strength of Muslim fanaticism in Pakistan, but also from the power of the Inter-Services Intelligence in Pakistan, which ran the Taliban in Afghanistan and managed the technology transfers of Pakistan's nuclear armoury. What is happening in Iraq naturally has repercussions throughout the Middle East, and this is what Hersh devotes his last chapter to explaining. 'Terrorism, instead of democracy,' he writes, 'is now spreading throughout the region.' It is a disturbing list. Syria, he believes, could have been won for American interests but was included by Bush in the 'Axis of Evil.' 'The Israelis are disaffected and seeking a risky new partnership with Kurdistan'. The Turks can tolerate this so long as Iraq remains intact. Prominent Saudis give money to Bin Laden. The Halliburton corporation, previously headed by Vice-President Dick Cheney, operates a number of subsidiaries in Saudi Arabia, and has established a dominant presence in Iraq. But the oil pipes in Iraq are being blown up. Water and petrol are in short supply in Iraqi cities and electricity supply is intermittent. In an Afterword written in March of 2005, Hersh writes that he does not expect an early improvement in the situation in Iraq, nor any recovery of George W. Bush from the unpopularity which now marks his Presidency.

Michael Barratt Brown

Robert Fisk Defending Civilisation

Robert Fisk, *The Great War for Civilisation: The Conquest of the Middle East*, Fourth Estate, 1,366 pages, hardback ISBN 1 84115 007 X, £25.00

Those familiar with Robert Fisk's reportage in *The Independent* will not be surprised by the passion of this book and its commitment to the truth as observed first hand. In an age of the 'embedded' and 'hotel' journalist, reporting from the Arab street is not for the faint-hearted, and the content of his work testifies to his own bravery and ability. The 29 media personnel killed in Iraq alone in 2005 testify to the hazards of the occupation. The skills honed through his living and reporting in the area for nearly 30 years have given him the necessary qualities for accurately assessing and describing the forces at work in the Middle East. He has eschewed the normal shifts of location which are usual for the foreign correspondent and the attendant clambering up the greasy pole of perceived journalistic success.

The book is a long (1,283 pages without the references!), discursive mixture of the history of the Middle East since 'The Great War', and the related colonial powers' dispensations for the area, coupled with more recent reportage from the region. We start with Fisk's meetings with bin Laden: firstly in 1993 in Sudan and then in 1997 in his Afghan mountain fastness round the campfire where the leader of 'world terrorism' attempts to recruit the author as a follower – a difficult situation for our intrepid journalist, given the remoteness and potentially violent surroundings. He manages to decline the offer with remarkable adroitness and care. Bin Laden, at this time, was fixated with the corruption and servility of the Saudi rulers to the Americans and the consequent US troops stationed in the 'Land of the Prophet', which made him determined to 'turn the United States into a shadow of itself'. No surprises there then – but Fisk's vignette of the character of the 'leader of world terrorism' is the most objective and interesting that we are likely to get for the foreseeable future. The re-visiting of Afghanistan provokes a return to Fisk's earlier reporting of the Russian intervention as well as earlier British intrusions. The brutal and hopeless nature of these conflicts is described with all its portents for the later American invasion and occupation. Fisk holds all this together with linked historical and even family-related asides that are typical of the whole book. This style has been criticised by some on the grounds of its sprawling nature, but such asides are usually stimulating and at times poignant.

An interesting chapter on Iran covers the overthrow of the Mossadeq government and the activities of both the British and American intelligence services, led respectively by 'Monty' Woodhouse and Kermit Roosevelt. The coup established American primacy in the Shah's Iran and consequently over its vast oil resources, with Britain coming a grateful second in ranking. The murderous Savak with its 60,000 operatives was to underpin the Shah's profligate and brutal rule until the 'Islamic Revolution' of 1979. Fisk has interviewed (sitting at the feet of) both Khomeini and Hojatolislam Khalkhi, the so-called 'hanging judge' of the new Islamic state, and the subsequent pages make chilling reading as Khalkhi cuts a swathe through not only remnants of the Shah's regime, but any murmurings of opposition, from schoolgirls to leaders of the Tudeh (communist) party. Conterminous with internal terror is the mass slaughter of the eight-year long Iran/Iraq war, a war which Fisk views from the frontline of both contending armies. And hair-raising reading it makes, too, with tales of Iranian child soldier martyrs and Iraqi poison gas attacks.

Fisk documents the connivance of the Western powers and the Soviet bloc in feeding the fires of war by supplying either Iran or Iraq (or both) with chemical, biological and conventional weapons. America's coaxing of Saddam's initial invasion of Iran and its supply of satellite information on Iranian frontline troop disbursements is also catalogued. Further American involvement is illustrated by the destruction of an Iranian passenger aircraft, on a regularly scheduled flight-path to Dubai, by ground-to-air missiles from the US warship *Vincennes*, demonstrating an abysmal lack of 'command and control' structures on the US ship. Fisk at the time thoroughly investigated and exposed this issue, but the story was distorted editorially by *The Times* and this episode is recalled in the book. This is a particularly good example of Fisk is at his most incisive, getting to the bottom of what actually happened, cutting his way through the deliberate obfuscation of military and political spokesmen and the inherent assumptions of an ever-cooperative media. It was the occasion for his final parting with the Murdoch-owned *Times*. One gets the feeling he relishes the investigative element of the correspondent's role, telling the truth, and where possible confronting those involved. He does this with the manufacturer of the US 'Hellfire' missiles, fired from an Israeli Apache attack helicopter at an ambulance in South Lebanon in 2000. The ambulance, clearly marked, was carrying women and children, many of whom were killed. The arms industry in general gets a whole chapter of condemnation and exposure for its record in intensifying and exacerbating Middle Eastern suffering. Additionally, the reporting of the on-going conflict in Israel and the occupied territories contains some of the most graphic descriptions of violence in the book. Grimly he brings the reality of the conflict, in all its brutality, sharply into focus, both Palestinian and Israeli, but never forgetting the inherent inequality of the struggle and the profound injustice and suffering perpetrated on the Palestinian people.

The chapters on Iraq reiterate a lot of what is already known about the brutality of the Saddam regime: the appalling treatment of the Kurds, Shia Muslims, Marsh Arabs and virtually any opposition, as well as the dreadful cost in Iraqi lives of the

Iran War, the Gulf War and the 2003 invasion and occupation. Fisk catalogues the cruelty of the pre-invasion sanctions policy and its dreadful consequences for the children of Iraq, as well as highlighting the terrible results of the use of depleted uranium in terms of cancers and birth defects. Once again here he is, at his campaigning, investigative best, exposing the cost of the wrong kind of Western intervention in the Middle East and its impact on the ordinary people of the area.

Many other matters are covered: the Armenian Genocide, the Kurds, the Algerian civil war, the betrayal of the Shiite US-provoked revolt at the conclusion of the first Gulf War, Sabra and Chatila, 9/11 and the second invasion of Iraq, the bombing of Afghanistan and much more. One constantly feels Fisk's urgency to get the alternative narrative into the public domain. His virtually monthly speaking tours of the United States, his appeals for medical funding for the sick depleted uranium affected children of Iraq in the columns of *The Independent,* and much else besides testify that this is a man in a hurry, driven by the clear moral imperative to confront the world with the suffering of Iraqis, Iranians, Palestinians, and all the affected peoples of the Middle East. This suffering is exacerbated (and often largely caused) by Western intervention and its accompanying thirst for oil. Therefore, in my opinion, Fisk must be forgiven for any criticism on the grounds of length and connectedness. He wanted to get it all on the record (using all 328,000 individual documents he has collected over the years) because it deserves to be on the record. This book is a very gruelling read and at times quite harrowing, but we all need to realise or re-confirm the consequences of what is time and again being done by our governments in our name.

John Daniels

Shia Uprising

Mark Etherington, *Revolt on the Tigris: The Al-Sadr Uprising and the Governing of Iraq*, C Hurst & Co Publishers Ltd, 252 pages, hardback ISBN 1850657734, £15

This is an insider's view, which offers a rare insight into the mess which was left behind after the bombing and occupation of Iraq in 2003. Mark Etherington was a former paratrooper in the British Army, born and raised in the Middle East, who had post-conflict experience in Yugoslavia, and was sent by the British Foreign Office to establish a new administration in the southern province of Wasit on behalf of the Coalition Provisional Authority (CPA) in preparation for Iraqi self-government. Etherington from the start disliked the 'quasi-colonial' status of an 'invasion force turned occupiers'. In particular, he questioned the responsibility of the military for overseeing the police and judiciary. He was not provided with a legal expert to review their working, and his American colleagues seemed to regard this as unnecessary; they had no doubts about their legal rights. Yet

Etherington's Balkan experience had taught him that without establishing the rule of law, civil reform is wellnigh impossible.

The absence of a recognised rule of law was not the only problem faced by his Coalition Provisional Authority unit. It was far too small to be effective in a province of nearly a million people, spread over a territory 120 km long by 110 km wide. Military security was supplied by a Ukrainian force which had rules of engagement of a peace-keeping and not a defensive nature. All other aspects of security and so-called 'life support', including local staff recruitment, were the responsibility of the contractors, Kellogg, Root and Brown, a company of the Halliburton group, of which Vice-President Dick Cheney had been chief executive.

Corruption was endemic, and this started from the highest levels of local government, such as it was, and worked downwards, via tribal, family and political party channels. Most serious of all, while Saddam's dictatorial regime had been replaced by a free for all, the infrastructure of the country – roads, bridges, electricity, water, sewerage and fuel supplies – had been destroyed by the bombing and not repaired. This, together with the disbanding of the army and the police, had left a mass of unemployed, widespread poverty, and profoundly disaffected young people.

This was the background to the uprising led by Moqtada al-Sadr in 2004, and the expulsion in a sixteen-hour fire-fight of Etherington and his CPA unit from their base in Kut. This was not an uprising of Sunnis and Ba'athists, one-time rulers of Saddam's Iraq, but of Shia. The Al-Sadr militia were only able to dominate the situation because of the universal anger at the failure of all public services – electricity, water, sewerage and fuel supplies – which had not failed under Saddam, and the universal lawlessness. 'You have conquered our country;' said one civil official to Etherington, 'it is your duty to protect us.' The province of Wasit lies to the east along the border with Iran and movement across the border is normally large-scale and continuous. Insurgents from Iran were often blamed by the Coalition for the uprising, but Etherington discounts this. Several of the border crossings had been closed and there were enough of the local population with arms from the disbanded forces to give al-Sadr his well-armed militia.

The reoccupation by American arms of Kut and the return of Etherington's unit were achieved by the employment of massive American fire-power. The death toll of al-Sadr's force has to be estimated in the thousands. Peace was re-established and new men installed in the local police force and civil government, but at the price of the retention of a continuous large-scale US military presence which has not prevented, has indeed probably encouraged, the suicide bombing of military targets.

While the whole infrastructure of the country remains unrepaired from the American bombing, it is hard to imagine from Etherington's description how any military withdrawal will occur. Tacitus' famous words about Roman rule apply: 'They make a wilderness and they call it peace.'

MBB

Lack of Intelligence

Crispin Black, *7-7 The London Bombs: What Went Wrong?*, **Gibson Square Books, 96 pages, paperback ISBN 1903933714, £5.95**

There has been remarkably little clarification of what the British authorities knew or didn't know in advance of the tube bombings and bus bombing in London on 7 July 2005. Charles Clarke protested at the time that nothing was known. Crispin Black records that both the French and Saudi authorities have claimed they knew in advance that attacks were planned. Indeed, the Saudis took some trouble in trying to alert the British authorities, but to no discernible effect, it seems. It was also said at the time that the Israelis had some prior notice, and that Benjamin Netanyahu, visiting London at the time, was warned to stay in his hotel next to Liverpool Street station, not far from the Aldgate bomb.

Certainly, Mr. Blair's Government has set its face against any public inquiry into these events. Nor has there been any convincing explanation as to why MI5's Joint Terrorism Analysis Centre (JTAC) – which 'analyses all intelligence relating to international terrorism, at home and overseas' and 'produces assessments of threats and other terrorist-related subjects' – lowered the official state of alert five weeks prior to the London bombings.

Crispin Black asks some pertinent questions, but offers little in the way of any substantial answer to that posed in his sub-title. A career in spookery (Cambridge, Sandhurst, Northern Ireland, Cabinet Office, and now 'independent intelligence analyst') leads Mr Black to urge the merger of international and domestic intelligence agencies in the United Kingdom, arguing that the distinction no longer corresponds to the reality of the work in which they are engaged. He goes on to describe the 'new strategic reality' in which British Muslims were 'prepared to kill their fellow countrymen in the cause of jihad'. Already, the consequences of that perception are keenly felt by Pakistani and other ethnic minority communities subject to increased surveillance, not to say harassment, by local police forces.

We always knew that the secret services were inimical to democracy. That they are also hugely incompetent should not, perhaps, come as any great surprise. They remain part of the problem, not part of the solution. For that we have to look to each other for some measure of mutual protection in this protracted period of gross political deceit and manipulation, when wars are seeded and prosecuted, and those who are responsible break international law apparently with impunity.

Tony Simpson